Try my Bible Quiz

Bruce Benson

Heart Wish Books

Try my Bible Quiz

Text copyright © 2024 Bruce Benson

All rights reserved

This includes the right to reproduce any portion of the text in any form

Published by Heart Wish Books
Cambridge, Massachusetts

heartwishbooks@gmail.com

Photo on page 42, courtesy of Apple

All Bible quotations are the author's paraphrase unless marked

Scripture quotations marked (KJV) are from the King James Version in the public domain

ISBN: 978-0-9998039-1-2

Other books by Bruce Benson

AHA moments from the Bible

Jehovah's Witnesses Hate Jehovah

The Bible on Abortion: The shedding of innocent blood

Gay-affirming theology: An explicit exposé

The Catholic Church: femme fatale

Bible Talk: 50 literal drawings explained

Speaking in tongues: Shamana bo-ho roe-toe

Joseph Reflects Jesus: Lifegivers

Other books by the author in Spanish

Momentos AJÁ de la Biblia

Los Testigos de Jehová odian a Jehová

La Biblia sobre el Aborto: El derramamiento de sangre inocente

Teología de la validación gay: Una exposición explícit

La Iglesia Católica: Mujer fatal

Charla sobre la Biblia: 50 dibujos literales explicados

¡Prueba mi cuestionario bíblico!

Hablar en lenguas: Shamana bo-jo ro-to

José refleja a Jesús: Dadores de vida

This book at a glance

Page 23: Introduction

Page 25: Teach salvation in 5 questions

Page 29: Ten questions to ask someone who says they're a Christian

Page 37: Jesus had a flock of sheep

Page 43: The Quiz questions

In the past, I hired a woman to do two things I don't know how to do. But I decided not to do that anymore. So, I can't list the title of this book or future titles in the "Other books by … " page of all my other books. But you can find my books if you google Bruce Benson Amazon or Bruce Benson Heart Wish Books.

She also put the page numbers in the right place, in the header at the top of the page. This time, I placed the page numbers myself, wherever. I made them bold and underlined, like this: **275**.

This is a homemade book. It was created by one guy sitting at a desk. Learn to see beauty in imperfections.

The next 17 pages are a guide to help you find what you're looking for.

The introduction is on page 23.

Introduction ... 23

365
He only lived **365** years ... 377, Q122

666
Two times the number **666** appears ... 195, Q77

Abandon
Who does God **abandon** in Romans 1:26-27? ... 151, Q54

Abortion
Should a 12-year-old **rape survivor** be given an **abortion**? ... 119, Q40

ACAB?
Are all **cops** bad? ... 139, Q49

Actually
Did Jesus **actually die**? ... 32

Alone
Why it's better to **not be alone**, Ecclesiastes 4:9-12 ... 287, Q103

Angels
He had the **face of an angel** ... 271, Q98

Can humans eat **angels' food** and vice versa? ... 345, Q117

Angry
Six times **Jesus** gets **angry** ... 435, Q129

Apostles
Did the apostles **steal corn**? ... 311, Q111

The two of the 12 **apostles** the Bible says were **executed** ... 191, Q75

He was the **first** apostle ... 171, Q64

The apostles **rejoiced** because they were **beaten**. Why? ... 287, Q104

Which of the 12 apostles was a **thief**? ... 201, Q79

Who **told** the **apostles** that Jesus **rose** from the dead? ... 79, Q21

Apple
Who bit the **apple** first, Adam or Eve? ... 107, Q34

Ark
The three things kept inside the **Ark of the Covenant** ... 213, Q82

How many of each animal did **Noah** lead into the **ark**? ... 151, Q53

Ask
If you lack _____, **ask God** for it, James 1:5 ... 299, Q107

Believe
Ten questions to ask someone who **says they believe** in Jesus ... 29

Beware
Beware, **don't let anyone** _____ you. – Jesus, Matthew 24:4 ... 63, Q12

Bible
Is the Bible the **only Scripture**, the only Holy Book? ... 32,68

Do you **study** the Bible **on your own**? ... 23,34

Birth of Jesus
The **town** where Jesus was **born** ... 75, Q17

Blessed

2 called **blessed** among women ... 183, Q71

Jesus said they're **more blessed** than His mother ... 337, Q115

Blind

The only two who **gave sight** to someone who was **blind** ... 359, Q119

Borrow

What does it means when a nation **borrows** money? ... 259, Q92

Bread alone

He said people don't live by **bread alone** ... 179, Q69

Buried

The only person **God** Himself **buried** ... 241, Q87

Who **buried Jesus**? ... 303, Q108

Children

God said *they* must shape **children's worldview** ... 47, Q2

How many of **Jacob's** (Israel's) **children** can you name? ... 79, Q22

Church

Is there a **Black** Church and a **White** Church? ... 209, Q81

Who **builds** the Christian **Church**? ... 107, Q35

Jesus cleanses the **Church** by the **washing** of water with __ ... 171, Q65

Coat

Three times one or more **brought a coat** to someone ... 365, Q120

Three who had a **coat** of **many colors** ... 351, Q118

Cops

Are all **cops** bad? ... 139, Q49

Creator
When should you **remember** your **Creator**? ... 51, Q3

Crucifixion
Who carried Jesus' **cross** to the place of His **crucifixion**? ... 51, Q6

How many **times** did Jesus **fall** when He carried His cross? ... 67, Q13

Nine times the OT **predicts Jesus' crucifixion** ... 491, Q135

Cry
Why I love to see **women cry** ... 267, Q95

Death
Did Jesus **actually die**? ... 32

The sign God gave to show that **Jesus defeated death** ... 107, Q36

Who's **responsible** for the **death** of Jesus? ... 543, Q141

When you **die**, your **soul returns** to ____ , Ecclesiastes 12:7 ... 103, Q32

devil, the
One who was **deceived by the devil**, and one who wasn't ... 463, Q132

Different ending
Gal. 6:15, 1 Cor. 7:19, Gal 5:6: **same start, different** ending ... 131, Q46

Don't look back
Three instances when **escapees** are told – **don't look back** ... 455, Q131

Earth
Did God create the **Earth without form** and void? ... 539, Q140

Eat
Can humans eat **angels' food** and vice versa? ... 345, Q117

Two times **Jesus** tells people to **eat Him** ... 275, Q100

Three who got **pleasure** from **eating** God's Word ... 279, Q101

Egypt
Which **book** of the Bible tells of **Israel's** exodus from **Egypt**? ... 59, Q10

Emmanuel
Jesus is called Emmanuel. What does **Emmanuel** mean? ... 75, Q18

Encouragement
Words of encouragement **said six times to Joshua** ... 147, Q51

Exodus 9:16
Who did God say **Exodus 9:16** to? ... 195, Q78

Face
He had the **face of an angel** ... 271, Q98

Faith
You receive salvation through **faith**, which comes by _____ ... 159, Q57

Can you **believe** in Jesus and **not be saved**? ... 159, Q58

Do you just believe **someone who says** they're a Christian ... 29

Famine
God said He will **send a famine** of _____, Amos 8:11 ... 191, Q76

Father
Who was **David's** father, **Solomon's** father, **Jesus'** father? ... 485, Q134

He is called **Holy Father** ... 267, Q96

Who is the **father** of the **Jews**? ... 167, Q63

Feet
When **Jesus** returns, where will **His feet** touch first? ... 123, Q43

Finger
Three times something was **written** by the **finger of God** ... 405, Q126

First and last
Two who said, "I am the **first** and the **last**." ... 71, Q15

First thing
The first thing God said **was not good** ... 83, Q23

The **first thing** Jesus said in the **Sermon on the Mount** ... 71, Q14

Five
Five-word statement made three times in **James 2:14-26**... 263, Q94

Isaiah 9:6 says **Jesus** will be **called** these **five names** ... 75, Q19

Jesus **prayed five times** that His followers be this, John 17 ... 167, Q60

Teach salvation in **five** questions ... 25

Four
Four times Jesus **favored the right** over the left ... 245, Q88

The **four words** written on the **high priest's hat** ... 187, Q74

Four things Jesus wants you to do to **people who hurt you** ... 175, Q68

Four things the book of **Proverbs** calls a **tree of life** ... 91, Q27

4 men who found a **wife** at a well (one was found for him) ... 385, Q124

Friend
Jesus said you're **His friend** if you do this ... 59, Q11

Gabriel
OT man and NT woman **Gabriel** told about Jesus' birth ... 315, Q112

Girl-like ewe
He loved a girl-like **ewe** ... 135, Q47

Gnashing
Two instances of **gnashing** of teeth ... 171, Q66

Goat
Can a **goat go to Heaven?** ... 163, Q59

God
Is **Jesus** God? ... 32

God's Word
Three who got pleasure from **eating God's Word** ... 279, Q101

Greatest person
Jesus called him the **greatest person on Earth** ... 311, Q110

Greek alphabet
The two letters of the **Greek alphabet** that Jesus said He is ... 43, Q1

Groan
Three who **groan** in Romans chapter 8 ... 255, Q90

Hammer
Three who were **handy with a hammer** ... 371, Q121

Hate
Two times **Jesus hates** ... 271, Q99

Four times Jesus tells **Christians to hate** ... 449, Q130

Herod Agrippa I
Why did God **kill** king **Herod Agrippa I**? ... 115, Q39

High priest's hat
The four words written on the **high priest's hat** ... 187, Q74

Holy Father
He is called **Holy** Father ... 267, Q96

Holy Life
If you try to live a **holy life like Jesus**, you will ____ ... 155, Q55

Holy Spirit
God living **within** the Christian ... 30

Who tells you what to do – a pastor, or **God's Holy Spirit**? ... 34

How I know
How I know **you know God exists** ... 99, Q30

Humble
Two who called **themselves humble** ... 111, Q38

Introduction ... 23

Jacob
How many of **Jacob's** (Israel's) **children** can you name? ... 79, Q22

James 2:14-26
Five-word statement made **three times** in **James 2:14-26**... 263, Q94

Jericho
The last thing Israel did before God collapsed **Jericho's** walls ... 91, Q26

How many times did **Israel walk around** Jericho? ... 91, Q26

Jesus
Six times Jesus **gets angry** ... 435, Q129

Who told the **apostles** that **Jesus rose** from the dead? ... 79, Q21

Jesus said, **Beware**, don't let anyone ____ you, Matthew 24:4 ... 63, Q12

The town where **Jesus** was **born** ... 75, Q17

Who **buried** Jesus? ... 303, Q108

Jesus **cleanses the Church** by the washing of water with __ ... 171, Q65

Who **carried** Jesus' **cross** to the place of His crucifixion? ... 51, Q6

Two times **Jesus wears a crown** ... 259, Q91

The sign God gave to show that **Jesus defeated death** ... 107, Q36

Did **Jesus actually die** and literally rise from death? ... 32

Beware, don't let anyone _____ you. – Jesus, Matthew 24:4 ... 63, Q12

Two times **Jesus** tells people to **eat Him** ... 275, Q100

Jesus is called **Emmanuel**. What does Emmanuel mean? ... 75, Q18

How many times **did Jesus fall** when He carried His cross? ... 67, Q13

Four times Jesus **favored the right** over the left ... 245, Q88

When **Jesus** returns, where will **His feet** touch first? ... 123, Q43

The **first thing Jesus said** in the Sermon on the Mount ... 71, Q14

Isaiah 9:6 says Jesus will be **called** these **five names** ... 75, Q19

Jesus said you're **His friend** if you do this ... 59, Q11

Is Jesus **God**? ... 32

The 2 letters of the **Greek alphabet** that Jesus said He is ... 43, Q1

Four times Jesus tells **Christians to hate** ... 449, Q130

Two times **Jesus hates** ... 271, Q99

If you try to live a **holy life like Jesus**, you will _____ ... 155, Q55

Four things Jesus wants you to do to **people who hurt you** ... 175, Q68

This book tells of the revelation of **Jesus** as **King of Kings** ... 179, Q70

Two who **kissed Jesus** ... 579, Q143

A **lamb** is an animal. So, **why is Jesus** called a lamb? ... 477, Q133

Jesus is **Lord** ... 30

Jesus said no one has **greater love** than _____ ... 107, Q37

3 times **Jesus said "Me"** when He meant His followers ... 329, Q114

Jesus said, "My **mother and siblings** are _____ ." ... 95, Q28

True or false. The Bible says Jesus will be **called a Nazarite** ... 55, Q8

Three times someone **told Jesus not to** do something ... 397, Q125

Jesus prayed five times that His followers be this, John 17 … 167, Q60

Nine times the OT predicts Jesus' crucifixion … 491, Q135

Who's responsible for the death of Jesus? … 543, Q141

Did Jesus ever sin? … 30

Did Jesus sleep? … 291, Q105

How did the Israelites snub Jesus before Jesus was born? … 415, Q127

How many days did Jesus stay on Earth after He resurrected? … 55, Q9

One time, Jesus stood, not sat, at God's right hand. Why? … 187, Q73

Three things Jesus said to take … 321, Q113

I taught you all these things so you'd have _____ . – Jesus … 119, Q41

Did Jesus say He's a thief? … 511, Q136

The town where Jesus was born … 75, Q17

Jews
Who is the father of the Jews? … 167, Q63

Did the Jews kill Jesus? … 546-547

Joshua
Words of encouragement said six times to Joshua … 147, Q51

King of Kings
This book tells of the revelation of Jesus as King of Kings … 179, Q70

Kissed
Two who kissed Jesus … 579, Q143

Lazarus, the poor man
What mode of transport took poor Lazarus to Heaven? … 217, Q83

Liar
Who was the first liar? … 205, Q80

Light
Two Jesus called the **light of the world** ... 139, Q48

Lilith
Is there a woman named **Lilith** in the Bible? ... 175, Q67

Lived
He only lived **365** years ... 377, Q122

Who **lived longer**, Moses or Sarah? ... 103, Q33

He lived by the **sword** ... 155, Q56

Lord
Jesus is **Lord** ... 30

Lost property
If you find your **neighbor's lost property**, can you keep it? ... 87, Q25

Love
He loved a **girl-like ewe** ... 135, Q47

Jesus said no one has **greater love** than _____ ... 107, Q37

Man of war
Three called a **man of war** ... 103, Q31

Mary Magdalene
Was Mary Magdalene a **prostitute**? ... 71, Q16

Mary, the mother of Jesus
Jesus said they're **more blessed** than His mother ... 337, Q115

Jesus said, "My **mother** and siblings are _____ ." ... 95, Q28

Was Mary a **virgin** when she gave birth to Jesus? ... 30

"Me"
3 times Jesus said "**Me**" when He meant His followers ... 329, Q114

Mediator (Peacemaker), only
Who is the only mediator **between us and God**? ... 123, Q42

Money
True or false? The Bible says **money** is the root of all evil ... 167, Q61

Moses
Who lived longer, **Moses or Sarah**? ... 103, Q33

Aaron spoke better. So, why did God have **Moses lead**? ... 295, Q106

How many **zebras** did Moses take on the **ark**? ... 127, Q44

Mother and siblings
My mother and siblings **are** _____ , – Jesus, Luke 8:19-21, 95, Q28

Nazarite
True or false. The Bible says **Jesus** will be called a **Nazarite** ... 55, Q8

Could a **woman** take the vow of a **Nazarite**? ... 167, Q62

Noah
How many of each animal did **Noah** lead into the **ark**? ... 151, Q53

Not good
The first thing God said was **not good** ... 83, Q23

Numbers 25:11-13
Who is God talking about in **Numbers 25:11-13**? ... 341, Q116

Old Testament
Jesus divided the OT into these **3 parts**, Luke 24:44 ... 381, Q123

Palindrome
Twins whose **names form** a **palindrome** ... 95, Q29

Parade, be thrown one?
If you try to live a **holy life like Jesus**, you will _____ ... 155, Q55

Passover
When was the **final Passover**? ... 255, Q89

Peace peace
God said He will keep you in **perfect peace if** you do this ... 131, Q45

Personal item
Women donated this **personal item** for the tabernacle ... 75, Q20

Pray
Jesus **prayed five times** that His followers be this, John 17 ... 167, Q60

Predictions
Nine times the OT **predicts Jesus' crucifixion** ... 491, Q135

Queen of Heaven
Who is the **Queen of Heaven**? ... 221, Q84

Rainbows
What do **rainbows represent**? ... 87, Q24

Red Sea
He parted the **Red Sea** ... 143, Q50

Rejoiced
The apostles **rejoiced** because they were **beaten**. Why? ... 287, Q104

Remember
When should you **remember your Creator**? ... 51, Q3

Responsible
Who's responsible for **the death of Jesus**? ... 543, Q141

Resurrection
Who **told the apostles** that Jesus rose from the dead? ... 79, Q21

Did Jesus **literally rise** from death? ... 32

How long did **Jesus stay on Earth** after He **resurrected**? ... 55, Q9

Reverend
His name is **Reverend** ... 267, Q97

Right
Four times **Jesus favored the right** over the left ... 245, Q88

Romans 1:26-27
Who does **God abandon in Romans 1:26-27?** ... 151, Q54

Salvation
What you **must do if** you want Jesus to **save you from your sin** ... 26

Can you **believe** in Jesus and **not be saved**? ... 159, Q58

Teach **salvation in five** questions ... 25

You receive **salvation through faith**, which comes by _____ ... 159, Q57

Same start
Gal. 6:15, 1 Cor. 7:19, Gal 5:6: same start, **different ending** ... 131, Q46

Samson
Did Samson **commit suicide**? ... 563, Q142

Sarah
Who **lived longer**, Moses or Sarah? ... 103, Q33

Satisfaction
Be satisfied with **one, and not the other**, Jeremiah 9:23-24 ... 307, Q109

Scarlet
Three **scarlet strands** ... 241, Q86

Scripture
Is the Bible the **only Scripture**, the only Holy Book? ... 32, 68

Sermon on the Mount
The first thing Jesus said in the **Sermon on the Mount** ... 71, Q14

Sheep
Jesus had a **flock** of sheep ... 37

He loved **a girl-like ewe** ... 135, Q47

She said ...
She said, "I'll go **wherever you go** ..." ... 591, Q144

Sin
What **is** sin? ... 26

Did **Jesus** ever **sin**? ... 30

What is the **penalty** for **sin**? ... 26

Three who lived on **Earth sinlessly** ... 147, Q52

What did Jesus do so we can be **saved** from **the penalty for sin**? ... 26

What to do if you want **Jesus to save you** from sin's penalty ... 26, 30

Sleep
Did Jesus **sleep**? ... 291, Q105

Snub
How did the Israelites **snub Jesus** before He was born? ... 415, Q127

Soul
Is the **soul immortal**? ... 183, Q72

When you die, your **soul returns** to _____ , Ecclesiastes 12:7 ... 103, Q32

Spies
Two brave **women who protected** two good **spies** ... 515, Q137

Spiritual temperatures
3 groups of people with **different spiritual temperatures** ... 283, Q102

Stood
One time, Jesus **stood, not sat**, at God's **right hand**. Why? ... 187, Q73

Study
Do you study the **Bible on your own**? ... 23,34

Sword
He lived by **the sword** ... 155, Q56

Take
Three things **Jesus said to take** ... 321, Q113

Teach
Teach **salvation in five** questions ... 25

I **taught** you all these things **so you'd have** _____ . – Jesus ... 119, Q41

Temperatures
3 groups of people with **different spiritual temperatures** ... 283, Q102

Ten
Ten questions to ask someone who **says they believe** in Jesus ... 29

Thief
Which of the 12 **apostles** was a **thief**? ... 201, Q79

Did **Jesus** say He's a **thief**? ... 511, Q136

Town
The town where **Jesus was born** ... 75, Q17

Tree of life, a
Four things the book of **Proverbs** calls **a tree of life** ... 91, Q27

Twins
Twins whose names form a **palindrome** ... 95, Q29

Four **sets of twins** ... 225, Q85

Virgin
Was Mary a **virgin** when she **gave birth** to Jesus? ... 30

Whip
Who does **God whip**? ... 263, Q93

Who told?
Who told the **apostles** that **Jesus rose** from the dead? ... 79, Q21

Wife
Five wives who got their **husband to sin** ... 523, Q138

Two times God said a **man** is to do what his **wife wants** ... 55, Q7

4 men who found a wife at a **well** (one was found for him) ... 385, Q124

Without form and void
Did God create the **Earth without form** and void? ... 539, Q140

How do you say "**without form and void**" in Hebrew? ... 535, Q139

Women
2 books of the **Bible** named after **women** ... 51, Q4

2 called **blessed** among women ... 183, Q71

2 **brave** women who protected two good **spies** ... 515, Q137

Why I love to see **women cry** ... 267, Q95

Four Old Testament women in **Jesus' genealogy**, 51, Q5

Could a **woman** take the **vow** of a **Nazarite**? ... 167, Q62

Women donated this **personal item** for the tabernacle ... 75, Q20

The no less than 9 **women who taught** the Bible to men ... 419, Q128

She said, "I'll go **wherever** you go ..." ... 591, Q144

Zebras
How many **zebras** did Moses take **on the ark**? ... 127, Q44

Thank you for trying my Bible Quiz. Let's start with this one:

Should you be tortured on a rack because you thought of an interpretation that's different than your pastor's?

If you answered yes, you may be suffering from a serious condition that's affecting 3 in 4 Christians. It's called pastor-worship. Fortunately, there's a safe and effective treatment. It's a personal relationship with Jesus through your own independent Bible study. Ask your doctor about Bible study – Doctor Jesus, that is. If your pastor hasn't taught you how to do independent Bible study, then you're in a cult. A pastor is your servant, Matthew 20:25-28. It's not his place to tell you what to do, or what to think. He's a waiter. His job is to assist you by feeding you God's Word. The apostle Paul said he was a *hyperetes*, a Greek word that means a galley slave, an under-rower, 1 Corinthians 4:1.

We have an enemy who's powerful, sneaky, and deadly. The Bible calls him the devil. And he's winning the spiritual war because most people either ignore him or think he's a cool dude. We need to get armed and informed by studying the Bible with a humble heart. Most Christians are lumps on a log. Do you have time, freedom, peace, and safety? How long do you expect that to last? You could've been enslaved and forced to work eighteen hours a day, digging a canal with your hands. Stop wasting your precious freedom! Become a slave for the Lord Jesus.

God gave me the greatest gift – a love of Bible study. If I study for five hours, I feel like I've just gotten warmed up. I want to study eight or ten hours a day. As I study, I think of questions that teach a lesson. You'll often see me stopped on a sidewalk, or standing in the aisle of a supermarket, writing down a question I just thought of.

Those questions became the Bible Quiz I used to share God's Word on street corners. This is my latest effort to whet your appetite. I've chosen 144 of my questions, and given you over 250 wonderful works of art to add to your enjoyment. It's time you became a serious Bible student. God's power is in that Book. It can change your life in surprising ways. You have to do three things, Matthew 11:28-30.
Bruce Benson

Teach salvation in five questions. Answers on page 26. **25**

One) What is sin?

Two) In one word, what's the penalty for sin?

Three) What did Jesus do to make a way for us to be saved from the penalty for sin?

Four) What must you do to receive that salvation from Jesus?

      A) Get baptized in water.
      B) Join a local church.
      C) Do whatever the leaders of your church tell you to do.
      D) Trust in the sacrificial death of the Lord Jesus Christ.
      E) All of the above.

Five) What's the first thing Jesus told us to do? It's the first word He said when He started His ministry. What's the word?

26 Answers to Teach salvation in five questions.

One) What is sin?

Disobeying God's laws is sin, 1 John 3:4.

Two) In one word, what's the penalty for sin?

<u>Death</u>, of the body, and the soul, Matthew 10:28; Romans 6:23.

Three) What did Jesus do to make a way for us to be saved from the penalty for sin?

God Himself took the penalty for us. He died in our place. Innocent Jesus gave His life as a sacrifice for our sin by being nailed to a cross.

> Jesus was crucified to pay for our rebellion.
> He was beaten to take the guilt for our sins.
> Jesus took our punishment and gave us His holiness.
> We were saved by the whipping He endured for us.
> Isaiah 53:5

Four) What must you do to receive that salvation from Jesus?

> A) Get baptized in water.
> B) Join a local church.
> C) Do whatever the leaders of your church tell you to do.
> D) Trust in the sacrificial death of the Lord Jesus Christ.
> E) All of the above.

The answer is D, trust in the Lord Jesus Christ.

Five) What's the first thing Jesus told us to do? It's the first word He said when He started His ministry. What's the word?

Jesus said, "Repent," Matthew 4:17. It means you change your mind about your sin, and ask Jesus to save you from sin's penalty. It shows God that you have the genuine faith that's required to receive salvation.

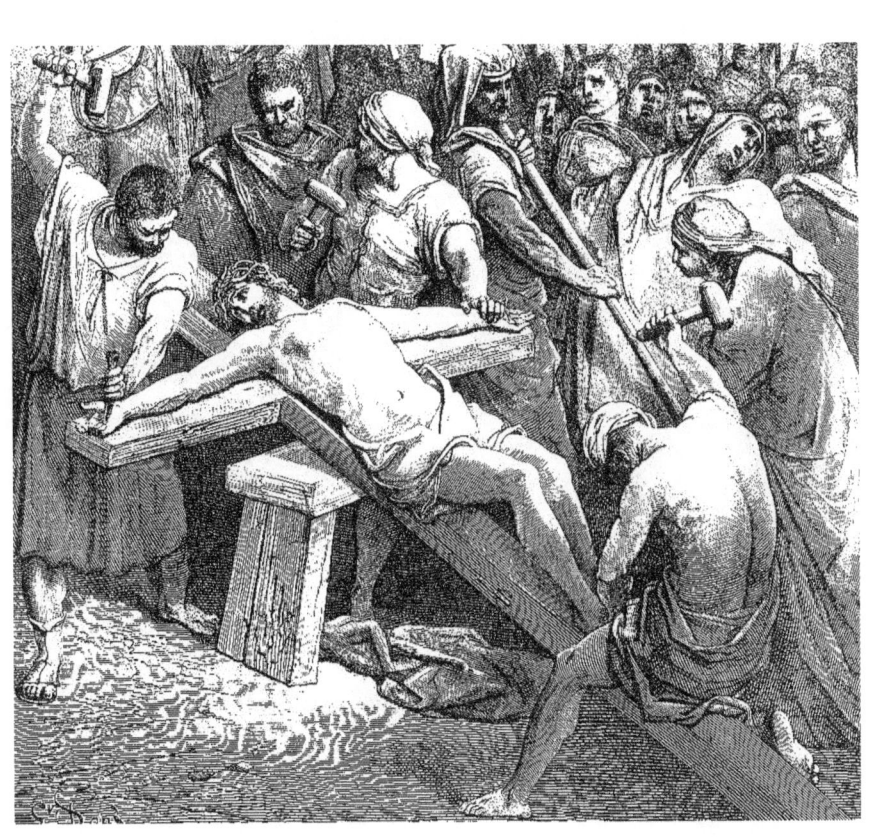

If someone says they're a Christian, do you just believe them? Yes? 29 What if later on they tell you Jesus comes down their chimney once a year and leaves presents under a tree? Do you still believe them?

I use the following 10 questions to expose the beliefs of someone who says they're a Christian. The answers start on page 30 .

One) Is Jesus Christ your Lord and Savior?

Two) If you answered yes to question one, my next question is, did you receive your salvation only through your faith, or by a combination of your faith and something you've done, such as baptism, or any other act, work, or deed? Or, are you completing your salvation by performing sacraments?

Three) Did Jesus give you His Holy Spirit to live in you?

Four) Was Mary a virgin when she conceived and gave birth to Jesus?

Five) Did Jesus ever sin?

Six) Is Jesus God?

Seven) Did Jesus actually die and literally rise from the dead?

Eight) Is the Bible the only Scripture, the only Authority, the only Umpire, the only Holy Book? Or, are other books also Scripture?

Nine) Do you study the Bible on your own?

Ten) Do you do what your pastor, church, or denomination tells you to do? Or do you do as God's Holy Spirit leads you?

30 Answers to 10 questions for someone who says they're a Christian.

One) Is Jesus Christ your Lord and Savior?

The Philippian jailer ran trembling to Paul and Silas. He fell on the ground and said, "Sirs, what must I do to be saved?" They said, "Believe in the Lord Jesus Christ and you will be saved, Acts 16:27-31. When you believe in Jesus as Lord, it means you want to obey Him.

Two) If you answered yes to question one, my next question is, did you receive your salvation only through your faith, or by a combination of your faith and something you've done, such as baptism, or any other act, work, or deed? Or, are you completing your salvation by performing sacraments?

Salvation is a gift from God that cannot be earned or completed by something we do. It can only be received through our genuine faith, Ephesians 2:8-9. God gives a complete, permanent salvation.

Three) Did Jesus give you His Holy Spirit to live in you?

If you don't have God's Holy Spirit living in you, then you don't belong to Jesus, you're not one of His, Romans 8:9; Ephesians 1:13-14.

Four) Was Mary a virgin when she conceived and gave birth to Jesus?

Mary herself testified that she was a virgin, Luke 1:34. And the angel Gabriel told her that Jesus will be conceived in her womb, not by a man, but by the power of God's Holy Spirit, Luke 1:35.

Five) Did Jesus ever sin?

Jesus never sinned and He never will. Jesus is eternally sinless.

> Jesus never sinned.
> And He never tricked anyone.
> 1 Peter 2:22

(Continued on page 32)

Believe in the Lord Jesus Christ, and you will be saved

Six) Is Jesus God?

Yes, Jesus is God, 100% God.

> God made Himself visible to us
> by being born in a human body.
> 1 Timothy 3:16

> Everything there is to God
> was in the human body that Jesus lived in.
> Colossians 2:9

Seven) Did Jesus actually die and literally rise from the dead?

Yes to both. Jesus told His disciples that He would be killed, and then rise from the dead after three days, Matthew 16:21. Jesus died on a wooden cross that He'd been nailed to, John 19:30. And three days later, Jesus rose from death, Matthew 12:40; 28:1-10; Revelation 1:18.

If you don't believe Jesus actually died and literally resurrected, then you're not a Christian, you're doomed, 1 Corinthians 15:12-20.

> If Jesus didn't rise from death,
> then believing in Him would be pointless
> because you'd still be in a state of
> condemnation because of your sins.
> 1 Corinthians 15:17

Eight) Is the Bible the only Scripture, the only Authority, the only Umpire, the only Holy Book? Or, are other books also Scripture?

The Bible is the only Scripture, the only Authority, the only Umpire, the only Holy Book, and there are no others, Acts 17:10-11.

We'll talk more about Acts 17:10-11 in the question, "When Jesus carried His cross to the place where He was crucified, how many times did He fall?" It's question # 13, on page 67.

(continued on page 34)

34 Nine) Do you study the Bible on your own?

When I say "study the Bible," I'm not talking about going to church services and Bible studies. Those are only there to help you with your own study. I'm talking about having an intimate relationship with Jesus through your own Bible study.

Do you have a place at home, at a desk or table, with bookcases full of books, where you can spend hours at a time immersed in Bible study? Do you get joy from your Bible study? Do you love it? Do you think about what you studied as you go through your day? When you wake up in the morning, do you feel like you can't wait to get to that desk?
Deuteronomy 6:6-9

If God hasn't given you a love of Bible study, you need to ask yourself if you're really a Christian. Jesus said His genuine disciples are those of us who keep our mind in His Word, John 8:31.

Ten) Do you do what your pastor, church, or denomination tells you to do, or do you do as God's Holy Spirit leads you?

I do as God's Holy Spirit leads me. I study, interpret, and teach the Bible. I don't let a pastor intimidate me, or steal from me. I trust what God's Holy Spirit teaches me. And I do the ministry God's Holy Spirit leads me to do. I don't let a pastor tell me to go stand on a street corner and hand out tracts. I use the gifts and abilities God gives me. I use my critical thinking, creativity, imagination, and uniqueness, to serve God.

> God gives us Christians a part of Him that lives in us.
> So, we don't need anyone to tell us what to do.
> 1 John 2:27

Suppose someone's considered to be the greatest living expositor of the Bible. But I have a different interpretation than him on a certain point. I don't say, "Well, he's the greatest expositor, and I'm just some nobody, so, he must be right and I must be wrong." No! I thank God for teaching me something the world's greatest expositor doesn't know. No, having an original thought is not the unforgivable sin – Ps. 119:99.

There are very evil people who call themselves Christians

They become members of fake Christian churches
Then they infiltrate the true Christian Church and the government

Jesus warned us about them. He told us to beware of bloodthirsty wolves who come to us in sheep's clothing, Matthew 7:15

37 **Sometimes I used this at my street ministry**:

Me: Jesus had a flock of sheep.

You: What?

Me: Jesus had a flock of sheep, out in a field. And they went, "Baa."

You: Is that so?

Me: Yes. One day, after Jesus rose from the dead, and before He went back to Heaven, He walked over to the sea of Tiberias, where some of His disciples were fishing. While they fished, Jesus prepared a meal of bread and fish over a fire. Then they all had breakfast together.
John 21:1-14

When they finished eating, Jesus took Peter aside and said to him, "Peter, do you love Me?" Peter said, "Yes Lord, You know I love You." And Jesus said, "Feed My lambs."

Then Jesus asked a second time, "Do you love Me?" Again, Peter said, "Yes Lord, You know I love You." And Jesus said, "Feed My sheep."

Then Jesus asked Peter a third time, "Do you love Me?" Peter was nearly out of his mind with grief now because Jesus asked a third time. Peter said, "Lord, You know everything. You know that I love You." And Jesus said, "Feed My sheep," John 21:15-17.

So, Jesus was saying, "Peter, I'm going back to Heaven soon, but I've got this flock of sheep out in a field, going, 'Baa.' And after I'm gone, I'll need you to take care of them for Me." Is that what Jesus meant?

You: No.

Me: No? Jesus doesn't have a flock of sheep in a field, going, "Baa"?

You: No

(Continued on page 40)

Jesus gives Peter the keys to the Kingdom of Heaven, Matthew 16:19

40 **Me**: Then who are the lambs and the sheep?

You: They're us.

Me: And by "us" you mean?

You: Christians, the followers of Jesus.

Me: Right!

By the way, I looked up the word "lamb" that Jesus used. It's #721 in the Strong's Concordance. It says it's a "lambkin." I looked up lambkin in Webster's New Universal Unabridged Dictionary. And Definition # 1 says it's a little lamb. But definition # 2 says it's someone who's exceptionally sweet, young, and innocent, as a young child.

Okay, so the sheep and the lambs are the followers of Jesus. That's who Jesus wants Peter to feed. So, Jesus is saying, "Peter, I need you to go back to work as a commercial fisherman, and catch a lot of fish, and feed them to My followers." Is that what Jesus meant when He told Peter, "Feed My sheep, feed My followers," to feed them fish?

You: No.

Me: Then what did Jesus want Peter to feed to His followers?

You: The Bible, the Word of God.

Me: Yes!

And it was so important to Jesus that after He goes back to Heaven, that Peter feed the Bible to His followers, that He staged that whole thing, asking Peter three times, "Do you love Me?" so Peter would know how important this was to Him, and so he would never forget. Jesus made sure Peter would obey Him. And he did obey. When the Church began, it was Peter who took the lead, and taught boldly.

Acts 1:15-22; 2:14-41;
3:1-26; 4:1-12; 5:1-11; 8:5-24; 10:1-48

The apostle Peter preaches boldly on the Day of Pentecost
Acts chapter 2

Q1) The two letters of the Greek alphabet that Jesus said He is.   **43**

44 A1) The two letters of the Greek alphabet that Jesus said He is.

> I am the Alpha and the Omega.
> Jesus, Revelation 1:9-18

Alpha and Omega are the first and last letters of the Greek alphabet.

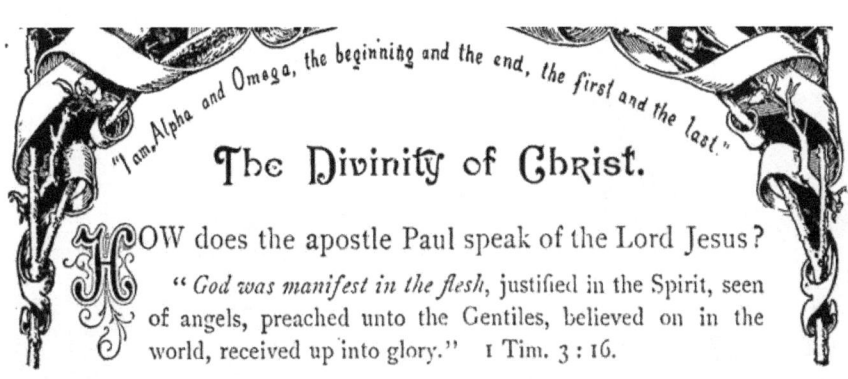

"I am Alpha and Omega, the beginning and the end, the first and the last."

The Divinity of Christ.

HOW does the apostle Paul speak of the Lord Jesus?

"*God was manifest in the flesh*, justified in the Spirit, seen of angels, preached unto the Gentiles, believed on in the world, received up into glory." 1 Tim. 3 : 16.

Q2) Multiple choice.

God said *they* must shape children's worldview:

        A) Parents
        B) Churches
        C) Government
        D) Schoolteachers

48 A2) Multiple choice.

God said *they* must shape children's worldview:

> A) Parents
> B) Churches
> C) Schoolteachers
> D) The government

The answer is A, parents.

When I was in high school in the late 1960s, boys started growing their hair long. I asked my mother if I could do that. She responded with an emphatic, "No!" I didn't understand why she said no, or why she took it so seriously, but I do now. And I'm glad she said no.

God said parents must etch His laws into the minds of their children.

> From this point on, you are to keep your mind on My words.
> Meditate on the commandments I'm giving you today.
> Sharpen My words in your mind.
> And use them to pierce your children's mind.
> Teach My words diligently to your children.
> Speak My words when you're sitting in your house,
> when you walk down the street, when you go to bed at night,
> and when you get up in the morning.
> God, Deuteronomy 6:6-7

I didn't know back then that the new trend of men wearing long hair was part of the devil's plan to feminize men and blur the differences between male and female. "It's disgraceful for a man to have long hair," 1 Corinthians 11:14. If I could tell my mother what's going on now, she'd think I have a wicked imagination. What started in the sixties as men with long hair, has turned into an America where children can be given puberty blockers. Minor girls can decide, on their own, to have their breasts, uterus, and vagina, surgically removed. "God hates to see males try to be female and females try to be male," Deuteronomy 22:5.

(continued on page 50)

50 Girls can have their clitoris turned into a penis. Boys can undergo chemical castration, breast augmentation, and penile inversion vaginoplasty. They can get those procedures whether or not their parents approve. And if the parents try to stop it, they can have their children taken from them.

A man named Karl Marx let the devil use him to create an evil philosophy. The Neo-Marxists who've infiltrated America's government and schools have taken control of your children's mind. "Replace home education by social"– Karl Marx, *The Communist Manifesto*, (ch.2) They want to destroy the God-ordained family. "Abolition of the family!" – Karl Marx, *The Communist Manifesto*, (ch. 2).

But they're not really Marxists. Their god is the devil. Marxism is just one of the isms they're using to try and destroy Christianity so they can take over the world. To do that, they need to destroy the Christian nation, America. So, they go after the children. They defy God by turning the children against their parents. They undermine the Biblical values taught to children by Christian parents by exposing the children to porn, shattering their innocence by teaching them about anal sex. "Communism abolishes eternal truths, it abolishes all religion, and all morality." – Karl Marx, *The Communist Manifesto*, (ch. 2).

They're transforming America into an anti-God hellhole, where the government is god. It's all been explained in the Bible. They're paving the way for the one-world government, and one-world religion, whose god is the devil, Revelation 13:11-18. That's why they're destroying America's sovereignty with ungodly open borders. Even Heaven has a wall – you have to qualify to enter, Rev. 21:12,17. A lot of good people shed their blood, and gave their life so we in America could have freedom of speech and religion. But now, a fifth column is doing away with our freedoms by criminalizing misinformation and hate speech. "Men fight for liberty and win it with hard knocks. Their children, brought up easy, let it slip away again, poor fools. And their grandchildren are once more slaves." – D.H. Lawrence

If you think what's happening now is shocking, hold on, it will get much worse. Then Jesus will return. Set your heart on that.

Q3) When should you remember your Creator?

Q4) The two books of the Bible named after women.

Q5) The four women from the Old Testament who are listed in the genealogy of Jesus in Matthew chapter one.

Q6) When the Roman soldiers led Jesus to the place where He'd be crucified, who carried the cross Jesus would be crucified on?

52 A3) When should you remember your Creator?

Ecclesiastes 12:1-6 says you should remember your Creator when you're young, before the difficult years of old age, when you'll say, "Life has lost all its pleasure."

A4) The two books of the Bible named after women.

Ruth and Esther

A5) The four women from the Old Testament who are listed in the

    genealogy of Jesus in Matthew chapter one.

One) Tamar, from Genesis 38:6-30, listed in Matthew 1:3.

Two) Rahab, from Joshua 2:1-24; 6:17, listed in Matthew 1:5.

Three) Ruth, from the book of Ruth, listed in Matthew 1:5.

Four) Bathsheba, from 2 Samuel 11:1-5,26, listed in Matthew 1:6, where she's called, "the wife of Uriah."

A6) When the Roman soldiers led Jesus to the place where He'd be crucified, who carried the cross Jesus would be crucified on?
 • The Gospels of Matthew, Mark, and Luke, say a man from Cyrene, named Simon, carried the cross Jesus would be crucified on.
                                  Matthew 27:32; Mark 15:21; Luke 23:26

 • The Gospel of John says Jesus carried the cross He would be crucified on, John 19:17.

Is that a contradiction? No. Then, what's the answer? The answer is, both Simon and Jesus carried the cross.

Q7) Two times God said a man is to do what his wife wants.

Q8) True or false? The Bible says this about Jesus:

>He will be called a Nazarite.

Q9) After Jesus rose from the dead, how long did He stay on Earth before He went back to Heaven?

56 A7) Two times God said a man is to do what his wife wants.

One) Sarah told her husband Abraham to send away her servant Hagar and Hagar's son Ishmael. And God told Abraham to do everything his wife Sarah wants him to do regarding that matter.   Genesis 21:1-13; See also Genesis 18:1-15 and Genesis 16:1-16

Two) God said when a wife asks her husband to satisfy her sexual desire, the husband is to do what his wife wants (and likewise the wife for the husband). God said that regarding sex, the husband's body belongs to the wife, and vice versa, 1 Corinthians 7:1-5.

A8) True or false: The Bible says this about Jesus:

> He will be called a Nazarite.

That's false. The Bible does not say Jesus will be called a Nazarite.

The Bible says this about Jesus:

> He will be called a Nazarene.
> Mathew 2:23

A Nazarene is someone who lives in, or is from, the city of Nazareth. Jesus was called a Nazarene because He lived in Nazareth as a child.

A Nazarite is someone who takes the vow of a Nazarite, which is explained in Numbers 6:1-21. God made Samson a Nazarite from the time Samson was in his mother's womb, Judges 13:1-7,13-14.

A9) After Jesus rose from the dead, how long did He stay on Earth before He went back to Heaven?

Jesus stayed for forty days, Acts 1:1-3.

Q10) In which book of the Bible do we read about the children of Israel's exodus from Egypt?

Q11) Jesus said you're His friend if you do this.

A10) In which book of the Bible do we read about the children of Israel's exodus from Egypt?

Answer:

Exodus

A11) Jesus said you're His friend if you do this.

>You're My friend if you obey Me.
>Jesus, John 15:14

Q12) Fill in the blank.

In Matthew 24:3, the disciples asked Jesus what would be going on when it's almost the end of the world and He's about to return.

Jesus answered their question with a warning. It's the most important thing He wants *us* to know. Jesus said there's something we must never let anyone do to us. And it's something that's going on like crazy now.

Jesus said:

> Beware, don't let anyone _____ you.
> Jesus, Matthew 24:4

64 A12) Fill in the blank.

In Matthew 24:3, the disciples asked Jesus what would be going on when it's almost the end of the world and He's about to return.

Jesus answered their question with a warning. It's the most important thing He wants *us* to know. Jesus said there's something we must never let anyone do to us. And it's something that's going on like crazy now.

Jesus said:

> Beware, don't let anyone deceive you.
> Jesus, Matthew 24:4

But how do you know if someone's trying to deceive you? The apostle Paul told some Christians – I have lots of things to tell you about Jesus. But it's difficult for me to explain them to you because you've become lazy. And through lack of use, your ears have become dull, so you're no longer able to understand.

Paul said – Considering how long you've been Christians, you should be teaching the Bible by now. Instead, I have to teach you the ABCs of Christianity all over again. Mature Christians eat solid food. But I have to feed you milk. Those who only drink milk are ignorant babies. They're inexperienced and unskilled in the teachings of Jesus, the Way of salvation, Hebrews 5:11-14.

Paul went on to say that it takes constant use, daily practice and training, exercising our mind in the Word of God. When Christians do that, God rewards us with discernment. And with that God-given discernment, no one can deceive us, we can tell the true from the fake. Studying the Bible will give you wisdom – God's wisdom, that saves your soul, 2 Timothy 3:15-17.

Legions are being deceived because they think the pastor is infallible. And they think he has all the right interpretations. Hear what the pastor has to say. But do your own search for the right interpretations. Only Jesus is infallible. Be like Mary, the sister of Martha, Lk. 10:38-42.

Q13) When Jesus carried His cross to the place where He was crucified, how many times did He fall?

__68__ A13) When Jesus carried His cross to the place where He was crucified, how many times did He fall?

Did you say two? Three? You might want to sit down.

The idea that Jesus fell is taught by the Catholic church, from something called, "The Stations of The Cross."

The Catholic church publishes all of their teachings in a book called, "The Catechism of the Catholic Church." In paragraph 97, they say the Bible *and* their traditions make up a single deposit of the Word of God.

Did you get that? They say their "traditions" plus the Bible are the Word of God. Their traditions are teachings that come from them, *not* from the Bible. Jesus condemned that. He called them "traditions from men." Jesus said that when people add their traditions alongside the Bible, they take away the Bible's ability to save people, Mark 7:13.

There can't be two authorities. There can only be one. When the Catholic church tells its people that the traditions of the Catholic church, plus the Bible, are the Word of God, they're telling them that the Catholic church is the highest authority.

The apostle Paul went to the city of Berea, Acts 17:10. He taught the people there about Jesus, Acts 17:2-3. And after listening to Paul's teachings, the people of Berea immediately went to the Scriptures, the Bible, and studied, day after day, doing an exhaustive investigation.

Why? Because the Bible is the only Scripture, the only Authority, the only Umpire, the only Holy Book. There is no other. So, they went to the Bible to find out if the things Paul was teaching were true.

Acts 17:11-12

Nowhere in the Bible does it say Jesus fell when he carried His cross. That teaching is a tradition from men. So, it must be condemned.

Mary Magdalene worshiping God

Q14) The first thing Jesus said in the Sermon on the Mount. **71**

Q15) <u>Two</u> who said, "I am the first and the last."

Q16) Was Mary Magdalene a prostitute?

A14) The first thing Jesus said in the Sermon on the Mount.

> Blessed are the poor in spirit:
> for theirs is the kingdom of heaven.
> Jesus, Matthew 5:3 (KJV)

The word "blessed" means happy. And "poor in spirit" means humble before God. It means we admit that we're utterly hopeless and helpless. We fall on our knees at the cross. Then we're happy because Jesus forgives our sins, gives us His Holy Spirit to live in us, and promises us we're going to Heaven. So, in a way, we're already in Heaven.

A15) <u>Two</u> who said, "I am the first and the last."

 • God the Father said, "I am the first and the last." He said it three times, in Isaiah, 41:4; 44:6; and 48:12.

 • Jesus said, "I am the first and the last." He also said it three times, in Revelation 1:17; 2:8, and 22:13.

They're the only two who said it. And the only two who *can* say it. Why? Because only God can say it. The lesson I want you to learn from this question is that Jesus is God, God Himself, 100% God, the very God, living in a human body like ours.

A16) Was Mary Magdalene a prostitute?

No. Mary Magdalene was not a prostitute.

The Bible says Jesus drove seven demons, or evil spirit beings from her, Luke 8:2. The Bible does not say she was a prostitute. That's a lie made up by a man. It's an evil slander against Mary.

Humble people are happy

Q17) The town where Jesus was born.

Q18) It says in Matthew 1:23 that Jesus is called Emmanuel. And, that verse tells us what Emmanuel means? What does it mean?

Q19) Over 600 years before Jesus was born, it was written in Isaiah 9:6 that Jesus would be called these five names.

Q20) God told Moses to build the tabernacle. It would be God's house, the place where He would live and meet with His people. Moses asked the children of Israel to donate items he could use to build the tabernacle and its furniture, Exodus 35:4-29.

There was a group of women who were God's loyal soldiers. They would meet up at the entrance of the tabernacle. Those women all donated the same personal item, Exodus 38:8.

What was it?

76 A17) The town where Jesus was born.

Jesus was born in the little town of Bethlehem, Matthew 2:1-2.

The name Bethlehem means House of Bread.

> I am the Bread of Life.
> Whoever comes to Me will never hunger.
> Whoever believes in Me will never thirst.
> Jesus, John 6:35

A18) It says in Matthew 1:23 that Jesus is called Emmanuel. And, that verse tells us what Emmanuel means? What does it mean?

Matthew 1:23 says Emmanuel means God with us.

A19) Over 600 years before Jesus was born, it was written in Isaiah 9:6 that Jesus would be called these five names.

> For unto us a Child is born, unto us a Son is given ...
> and His name shall be called Wonderful, Counseller,
> The mighty God, The everlasting Father,
> The Prince of Peace.
> Isaiah 9:6 (KJV)

A20) God told Moses to build the tabernacle. It would be God's house, the place where He would live and meet with His people. Moses asked the children of Israel to donate items he could use to build the tabernacle and its furniture, Exodus 35:4-29.

There was a group of women who were God's loyal soldiers. They would meet up at the entrance of the tabernacle. Those women all donated the same personal item, Exodus 38:8.

They donated their mirrors, which at that time, were made of metal, Exodus 38:8. Moses used their mirrors to make the brass laver, or washbasin. It's where the priests washed their hands and feet before they worked in the tabernacle, Exodus 30:17-21; 40:30-32.

Q21) Who told the apostles that Jesus rose from the dead?

Q22) How many of Jacob's (Israel's) children can you name?

<u>80</u> A21) Who told the apostles that Jesus rose from the dead?

It was Mary Magdalene.

The resurrection of Jesus is the greatest, most significant event in the history of the world. And, who was the first person Jesus appeared to and talked to after He rose from the dead, the first one He let know that He was alive again? It was Mary Magdalene, Mark 16:9.

And, Jesus sent Mary Magdalene to tell His apostles that He rose from the dead, Mark 16:10-11; John 20:17-18.

Are you getting this? Those men, the apostles, were His closest associates for the three years of His ministry. But Jesus honored Mary Magdalene, a woman, to be the first person to know about the most important event in human history. And He let her be the one to announce it to the men who had been His closest associates.

A22) How many of Jacob's (Israel's) children can you name?

Did you say twelve? I have thirteen. Jacob had twelve sons who became the twelve tribes of Israel, Genesis 35:23-26. And Jacob had a daughter named Dinah, Genesis 30:21. Here they are in the order of their birth:

> Reuben
> Simeon
> Levi
> Judah
> Dan
> Naphtali
> Gad
> Asher
> Issachar
> Zebulun
> * Dinah
> Joseph
> Benjamin

Jesus rises from death and surprises Mary Magdalene

Q23) The first thing God said was not good.

In Genesis 1:2-31, God created everything. And seven times, He looked at what He'd created and said it was good. Genesis 1:4,10,12, 18,21,25,31

But in Genesis 2:18, God said something He'd created was not good. What was it?

84 A23) The first thing God said was not good.

In Genesis, chapter one, God created everything. And seven times, He looked at what He'd created and said it was good.   Genesis 1:4,10,12, 18,21,25,31

But in Genesis 2:18, God said something He'd created was not good. What was it?

It was Adam's singleness. God said it's bad for the man to be alone, Genesis 2:18. And I agree.

So, God created the woman, a complementary counterpart for the man, because he needs someone to help him. Look it up. The word is # 5828. It means someone who helps.

Yes, the word is also used for help from the Lord, Psalms 121:1-2. But, your wife isn't the Lord. And it was the Lord who said the woman was made for the man, 1 Corinthians 11:9. The Lord also said a husband is to love his wife like Jesus loves His wife, the Church. And Jesus gave His life for His wife, Ephesians 5:25.

I noticed something I want to share with you because I think you'll find it interesting like I did. In Genesis 2:17, God told Adam he will die if he eats from a certain tree. Then, in the very next verse, Genesis 2:18, God said it's bad for a man to be alone, so God made a woman for Adam.

But it was that very woman who got Adam to eat from the tree that God told him not to eat from, Genesis 3:6; 5:5.

Adam passed away today.
He was only 930 years old.
Adam was originally from Eden,
where he was working as a tiller
when he met Eve, the love of his life.
The cause of death was disobedience.

Adam and Eve are cast out of the Garden of Eden

Q24) What do rainbows represent? __87__

Q25) If you find your neighbor's lost property, can you keep it?

88 A24) What do rainbows represent?

God put people in flesh bodies and placed us here on planet Earth, Genesis 1:26-28; 2:5-8,18-25. He wanted to find out who will love Him, and show their love by obeying Him. John 14:21-24.

But Adam and Eve disobeyed God. They committed the first sin, Genesis 2:15-17; 3:1-24, 1 John 3:4. And because of that first sin, all humans are guilty of sin, Romans 5:19. The penalty for sin is death.
Romans 6:23;
1 Corinthians 15:21-22, 45-58

After Adam and Eve brought sin into the world, they had children, the human race. As time went on, God observed that the wicked things people did were becoming more and more depraved. Their minds were always coming up with evil thoughts and plans. It pained God. And He started having second thoughts about putting people on Earth in flesh bodies, Genesis 6:5-6.

God did find one descendant of Adam who was obeying Him. It was a man named Noah. God decided to kill every human, and every living thing on Earth by flooding the Earth with a great rain. He would only save Noah and his family. You've heard of Noah's ark. You can read about it in Genesis 6:7-22; 7:1-24; 8:1-22; 9:18-19.

After the flood, God told Noah that He would never again kill all living creatures with a flood. God said He will make a rainbow in the sky. And the rainbow will represent His promise that He will never again destroy all life on Earth with a flood, Genesis 9:8-17.

A25) If you find your neighbor's lost property, can you keep it?

No. It says in Deuteronomy 22:1-3 that when you find your neighbor's lost property, you cannot keep it. You must make every effort to get it back to them.

Corruit Hiericho totum cum circuit Urbem Arca Dei, voce et populi, et clangore tubarum.

Q26) A two-part question:

1) How many times did the children of Israel walk around the city of Jericho?

2) What was the last thing Israel did before God knocked down the walls of Jericho?

Q27) Four things the book of Proverbs calls a tree of life.

A26) A two-part question:

1) How many times did the children of Israel walk around the city of Jericho?

Did you say seven?

No. The children of Israel walked around the city of Jericho once a day for six days. Then, on the seventh day, they walked around Jericho seven times. So, they walked around Jericho thirteen times.
Joshua 6:5,20

2) What's the last thing Israel did before God knocked down the walls of Jericho?

Did you say blow the trumpets?

No. God said the priests are to blow the trumpets, and then, all the people, when they hear the trumpets, are to shout with a great shout, and then the wall of the city will fall down flat, Joshua 6:2-4.

A27) Four things the book of Proverbs calls a tree of life.

One) Wisdom is a tree of life for those who cling to her.
Proverbs 3:13-18

Two) The good work done by a righteous person is a tree of life to those who are willing to receive it, Proverbs 11:30.

Three) When the good work a righteous person sets out to do is accomplished, it is a tree of life, very satisfying, Proverbs 13:12.

Four) The good words spoken by a righteous person are a tree of life. They are a healing medicine to those who want to hear them.
Proverbs 15:4

Jesus is The Tree of Life

Q28) Fill in the blank:

One day, when Jesus was teaching a huge crowd of people, His mother came looking for Him, along with His brothers and sisters. But they couldn't get near Him because there were so many people listening to Him speak, Luke 8:19-21. Someone told Jesus that His mother and siblings wanted to see Him. And Jesus said:

>   My mother and siblings are _____ .

Q29) Twins whose names form a palindrome.

A palindrome is anything that's the same backward and forward, like the name Hannah, or the number 123454321.

96 A28) Fill in the blank:

One day, when Jesus was teaching a huge crowd of people, His mother came looking for Him, along with His brothers and sisters. But they couldn't get near Him because there were so many people listening to Him speak, Luke 8:19-21. Someone told Jesus that His mother and siblings wanted to see Him. And Jesus said:

> My mother and siblings are _____ .

Answer:

> My mother and siblings are the people who are
> actually listening to the Word of God.
> They're the ones who want to
> understand what God said, and obey Him.
> Jesus, Luke 8:21

A29) Twins whose names form a palindrome.

A palindrome is anything that's the same backward and forward, like the name Hannah, or the number 123454321.

Answer:

In Genesis 38:27-30, an Israelite woman, named Tamar, gave birth to twins, whose names are given there as Zarah and Pharez.

In Numbers 26:20 and 1 Chronicles 2:4, Zarah's name is spelled Zerah. So, if we put Zerah and Pharez side by side, they form a palindrome:

> ZERAHPHAREZ

You've got a pal in Drome.

My mother and siblings are those who are listening to the Word of God and obeying what God says

Q30) How I know you know God exists. **99**

100 A30) How I know you know God exists.

God said He's angry with you. He knows the reason you're denying His existence is because you want to go on disobeying Him.

You have no excuse. God said He's shown you all you need to see to know He exists. No, you can't see God Himself. But you can see Him in all the things He created, Romans 1:19-20.

But you won't honor God as God. You won't thank Him for all the good things He gives you. You want to hide in the darkness and avoid His light, John 3:19-21. Your reasoning is worthless. God will let you go your own way for a while. But the day will come when you'll have to face Him. There will be a judgment. And Jesus will either send you to Heaven or hell. You can decide which one you want. Matthew 13:47-51; Luke 13:1-5; Romans 1:18-22; 2 Thessalonians 1:7-10

No God? Stop for a second and think about the fact that you can think. Your brain is a hunk of meat. But God put a computer in it. That's why you have a sense of humor, self-awareness, the ability to laugh, love, create, cry, feel compassion, and solve problems. You don't have to make your heart beat or your lungs breathe. And your brain stores memories so you can call up images and feelings whenever you want.

We take our eyesight for granted. But eyesight is impossible. Think about your taste buds, your ability to feel pleasure and sing. God gives you that. And when the life God gives you leaves your body, it turns into a sack of dust, Eccl. 12:7.

The sun is a huge, super hot ball, millions of miles away. But it gives us a perfect summer day here on Earth. That's some kind of fine-tuning.

Ever wonder why you feel the way you do about the opposite sex? How about Grapes? The Big Bang created grapes? Yes, of course it did. It created the internet too. What about gravity and music, or the way a dog goes crazy when they see their person after a long absence?

(continued on page 102)

THE AGNOSTIC.

102 Why do birds sing and puppies play? Why do you want to save someone's life? Why does sunlight purify nature? Why do you dream when you're sleeping? The Big Bang has no idea. It can't think. It's just a stupid explosion.

God said He's given everyone sufficient evidence of His existence.
Acts 14:16-17

> The sky tells us about the splendor of God.
> It's God staring you in the face.
> Psalms 19:1

So, tell me, is this what you believe? The Big Bang came into existence, somehow, from nothing. It exploded and created the Earth. Water, too? An explosion of rocks made water? Then life? How did the first living creature get that spark of life? Where did the life come from? And then some bacteria and a polliwog evolved into a human being, with all the complexities of the human brain and body? Is that what you believe?

There's no such thing as nothing. If in the beginning there was nothing, there would still be nothing. You can't get something from nothing. Therefore, the cause of our existence has always existed.

An eternal God is the logical explanation. The intricacies of our universe and the human body had to be planned and created by a person with an amazing mind, and powers beyond our ability to comprehend. God created everything in our world when He declared, "Let there be ... ." It didn't come from nothing. It came from God.

Every physical thing decays and dies. If things go on as they are, all life on earth will die. The sun will burn out. Then what? What if this life *is* all there is? When you die, is that it for you ? Nothing? Yes, nothing. On the other hand ...

The Bible has a promise of forever, with the kindest, most generous person you'll ever meet, a loving God who feels compassion and pity, and longs to show mercy and forgiveness. He has always existed, and always will. He lives in another dimension, yet, He's very much like us.

Q31) Three called a man of war.

Q32) Fill in the blank:

> When you die, your soul returns to _____ .
> Ecclesiastes 12:7

Q33) Who lived longer, Moses or Sarah?

104 A31) Three called a man of war.

• Before David was the king of Israel, and before he served in the military, he was called a man of war, 1 Samuel 16:18. Then David killed Goliath, the giant Philistine, and cut off his head.   1 Samuel 17:33-37; See also 1 Samuel 17:45

• Goliath was called a man of war by king Saul, 1 Samuel 17:33.

• God parted the Red Sea so the children of Israel could pass through the sea and escape from the Egyptian army. When the Egyptian army also tried to pass through the sea, God made the waters return to kill the Egyptians. Then Israel sang the first song in the Bible.

Here's one of the things they sang:

> The Lord is a Man of war.
> The Lord (I am) is His name
> Exodus 15:3

See also Psalms 24:8.

A32) Fill in the blank:

> When you die, your soul returns to _____ .
> Ecclesiastes 12:7

When you die, your flesh body returns to the dust, where it came from. And your soul returns to God, where *it* came from, Ecclesiastes 12:7.

A33) Who lived longer, Moses or Sarah?

Moses lived 120 years, Deuteronomy 34:7.

Sarah lived 127 years, Genesis 23:1-2.

Sarah lived longer than Moses.

Q34) Who bit the apple first, Adam or Eve?

Q35) Who builds the Christian Church?

Q36) What miracle did God do immediately after Jesus died on the cross, as a sign that Jesus defeated death? And God didn't reveal the miracle to people until after Jesus rose from the dead.

Q37) No one shows greater love than the person who ____. – Jesus, John 15:13

A34) Who bit the apple first, Adam or Eve?

The Bible doesn't say Adam and Eve bit an apple.

God said they would die if they ate from the tree of the knowledge of good and evil, Genesis 2:17. He didn't say don't eat from an apple tree. You can read about apple trees and apples in Song of Solomon 2:3,5.

I ask this as a reminder to never assume that what you hear is true, and to always read the Bible carefully.

A35) Who builds the Christian Church?

God builds the Christian church.

> Every day, the Lord gathered
> the saved people into the Church.
> Acts 2:47

A36) What miracle did God do immediately after Jesus died on the cross, as a sign that Jesus defeated death? And God didn't reveal the miracle to people until after Jesus rose from the dead.

Immediately after Jesus died on the cross, graves opened up, and many of the bodies of Christians who died came to life. Then, after Jesus rose from death, they walked into Jerusalem, and many people saw them.
Matthew 27:52-53

A37) No one shows greater love than the person who ____. – Jesus.

> No one shows greater love than the person who
> lays down their life for their friends.
> Jesus, John 15:13

Q38) Two who called themselves humble.   <u>111</u>

112 A38) Two who called themselves humble.

One) Moses

> Moses was a very humble man,
> more humble than anyone in the whole world.
> > Numbers 12:3 (written down by Moses)

Two) Jesus

God hates it when we act proud. He loves humble people. We do wrong when we let pride make us sin. When we walk down the street, or drive, we should let other people go first. Oh, how good that feels.

Kings don't ride donkeys. But in Matthew 21:1-11, we see Jesus, the Creator of the universe, Colossians 1:12-20, the King of Kings, Revelation 19:16, humbly riding into Jerusalem on a donkey.

Being humble doesn't mean being weak. When Jesus got to Jerusalem, He went to God's house, the temple, and He saw people running businesses right inside the temple. Humble Jesus chased them all out. He took hold of the seats people sat on to sell doves, and threw them to the floor. Then He flipped over the money changer's tables.
> > Matthew 21:12-13

It doesn't mean we can do that. We can't. Jesus was *not* engaging in civil disobedience. He could do that because that was His house. He's God.

In Matthew 11:28-30, Jesus said He will put His arm around you and walk with you. He will teach you how to live your life like He did when He took on a flesh body like ours. He will let you rest from your futile effort to save yourself. Jesus said He is humble, and His arm is gentle. He said He will give rest to your soul. You can trust Him.

> Humble people are happy.
> They know I'll give them the earth.
> > Jesus, Matthew 5:5

> > > (continued on page 114)

114 Someone disrespects you and you burn with anger and want to get back at them. You're letting pride drive you mad.

Look at the example Jesus gave us. He was God Himself. He deserved all the respect in the world. But He was betrayed. People told lies about Him, Matthew 26:59-66. Jesus was found guilty of a death penalty offense that He didn't commit. He was executed in a cruel, humiliating way, stripped naked in public, spit on, punched and mocked, His flesh was torn by painful whipping, and then He was nailed to a cross. And Jesus was innocent, the most innocent person who ever lived.

Jesus could have erupted in anger. He could have tortured *them* to death. But He didn't. He took it. And He asked God to forgive them for doing that to Him. Jesus wasn't thinking about getting back at them. Jesus cared about them. He wanted them to be with Him forever in Heaven. And in the Bible, God commands us to do the same.

> If you say you're a Christian,
> then live your life like Jesus lived His.
> 1 John 2:6

For us to be able to live our life like Jesus, God has to humble us. We have to live a life of suffering. It hurts. We'll cry. We'll beg Him to stop. The Christian life is a crucible, not a cruise.   Isaiah 53:3; 1 Peter 2:21

But we Christians have an inner peace and joy that no one else has, John 14:27; Philippians 4:7; James 1:2-3. And after we've suffered for a while, God will fix everything, 1 Peter 5:10.

And we have God's promise of eternity in Heaven.   Ephesians 1:14;
1 John 5:13

Q39) Why did God kill king Herod Agrippa I?

A39) Why did God kill king Herod Agrippa I?

In Acts 12:1-2, we read that king Herod Agrippa I started doing evil things to the Christians living under his rule. He even killed one of the twelve apostles, James, the brother of the apostle John. Then he put the apostle Peter in prison and planed to kill him too. But during the night, when Peter was sleeping, God sent an angel to wake him up and lead him out of the prison and set him free, Acts 12:3-11.

One day, on a certain special occasion, king Herod Agrippa I arrayed himself in his royal robes, and sat on his throne, and began lecturing the assembled crowd. When the people heard Herod speak, they started shouting, "We're hearing the voice of a god, not a man."

At that very instant, an angel of the Lord struck Herod down because he tried to put himself in the place of God. Then Herod was eaten by worms, and he died. And the preaching of the Word of God continued more and more, Acts 12:21-24.

Q40) If a twelve-year-old girl is pregnant because she was raped, should she be given an abortion?

Q41) Fill in the blank:

> I taught you all these things so you'd have _____ .
> Jesus, John 16:33

120 A40) If a twelve-year-old girl is pregnant because she was raped, should she be given an abortion?

No. A twelve-year-old girl who's pregnant from rape must not be given an abortion. Isn't that cruel? She could die in childbirth. But if you give her an abortion, it's not a question of whether the baby in her womb could die. They *will* die.

God gives everyone the right to live, including children who happen to be in their mother's womb. God said – don't do murder, Exodus 20:13. God doesn't give anyone the right to murder a child in the womb, not even a twelve-year-old rape survivor.

Yes, it's awful. Either a child is murdered, or a child gives birth to a baby conceived by a man who raped her. That's the world we made.
Romans 3:23; 5:12

It's a self-evident and scientific fact that abortion is the murder of a person. Has there ever been a government that put murder to a vote? God created government to protect citizens from things like murder, rape, and theft.   Genesis 9:6; Leviticus 24:17;
Deuteronomy 17:6; Romans 13:1-7

We live in a sinful world. The battle over what the government does about abortion will be fought until the bitter end. It won't be resolved until Jesus returns and sets up His Kingdom, Daniel 2:44.

A41) Fill in the blank:

> I taught you all these things so you'd have peace.
> Jesus, John 16:33

On the night before He was crucified, Jesus told His apostles, and all Christians, that in this world, we will feel crushed by persecution and other troubles. But, Jesus said,

> Be courageous! I have defeated this world.
> John 16:33

Q42) Who is the only mediator (peacemaker) between us and God? **123**

        A) Mary
        B) Jesus
        C) Priest
        D) Moses

Q43) When Jesus returns to Earth, where will His feet touch down?

A42) Who is the only mediator (peacemaker) between us and God?

  A) Mary
  B) Jesus
  C) Priest
  D) Moses

The answer is B, Jesus.

> There is one God.
> And, there is one Mediator
> between us and God.
> He is the Man, Jesus Christ.
>   1 Timothy 2:5

A43) When Jesus returns to Earth, where will His feet touch down?

It says in Zechariah 14:4, that when Jesus returns to Earth, His feet will touch down in Israel, on the Mount of Olives, in God's city, the holy city, Jerusalem, Psalms 48:1-3.

"THERE IS NONE OTHER NAME UNDER HEAVEN GIVEN AMONG MEN, WHEREBY WE MUST BE SAVED"

Q44) How many zebras did Moses take on the ark?   **127**

128 A44) How many zebras did Moses take on the ark?

People liked to ask me that question when I did my street ministry. They were hoping I'd say, "two." Then they'd inform me that it was Noah who had the ark, not Moses. Well, the joke's on you funny guy. What my tormentors didn't know is that Moses had an ark too.

The children of Israel went to live in Egypt because of a famine. You can read about it in Genesis, chapters 37,39-47,50. Israel lived in peace in Egypt. They had a good relationship with the king and the people. Israel had lots of children, they were spreading to all parts, Exodus 1:7. But then a new king took over. He worried that Israel might join Egypt's enemies in a war against Egypt. So, he enslaved the Israelites.
Exodus 1:8-14

Then the king of Egypt ordered that every son born to an Israelite was to be thrown in the Nile river and drowned, Exodus 1:22.

A boy named Moses was born to Amram and his wife Jochebed, an Israelite couple living in Egypt, Exodus 6:20. Moses' mother perceived that he was beautiful to God, Exodus 2:2; Acts 7:20. In order to save his life she made him a little ark. She put Moses in the ark and hid him among the reeds on the banks of the Nile river, Exodus 2:3.

What was that ark that she put Moses in? Well, it's # 8392 in the Hebrew dictionary in the Strong's Concordance. It means a box. Someone else made an ark. Yes, Noah, Genesis 6:14. And guess what. The ark Noah made is also # 8392 – the same as Moses ark!

Though it's unlikely that Moses had room for two zebras on his ark.

There's a third ark in the Bible. It's the Ark of the Covenant. In this case the word, "ark," is # 727. But it also means a box, or a chest. The first mention of the Ark of the Covenant is in Exodus 25:10. It was one of the items in the Tabernacle, the place where God met with His people.

Pharaoh's daughter finds Moses in his little ark

Pharaoh's daughter holds Moses, as Moses' sister Miriam looks on while holding his ark

Q45) God said in Isaiah 26:3 that He will keep you in perfect peace, or as the original Hebrew says – peace peace – if you do this.

Q46) There are three verses that start by teaching us that when we belong to Jesus, being circumcised is nothing, and not being circumcised is nothing. And each of those verses ends by telling us what *is* everything. But they all say something different.

The verses are Galatians 6:15; 1 Corinthians 7:19; Galatians 5:6.

Fill in the blank.

- Circumcision is nothing. And uncircumcision is nothing. What is everything is _____ ,Galatians 6:15.

- Circumcision is nothing. And uncircumcision is nothing. What is everything is _____ , 1 Corinthians 7:19.

- Circumcision is nothing. And uncircumcision is nothing. What is everything is _____ , Galatians 5:6.

A45) God said in Isaiah 26:3 that He will keep you in perfect peace, or as the original Hebrew says – peace peace – if you do this.

God will keep you in peace peace if you show that you trust Him by keeping your mind set on Him. God said "peace" twice for emphasis.
Isaiah 26:3

It says in Philippians 4:7 that the kind of peace God gives is beyond all human understanding. It will guard your heart and mind. But you have to do your part. Stay close to Jesus. He's the Word of God, the Bible. If you want that peace from God, then study the Bible seriously, be immersed. Keep your mind set on God by keeping it in the Bible. But you have to have the right heart – you have to want to obey God.

A46) There are three verses that start by teaching us that when we belong to Jesus, being circumcised is nothing, and not being circumcised is nothing. And each of those verses ends by telling us what *is* everything. But they all say something different.

The verses are Galatians 6:15; 1 Corinthians 7:19; Galatians 5:6.

Fill in the blank.

When you belong to Jesus:

- Circumcision is nothing. And uncircumcision is nothing. What is everything is that God created you as a new person because you've given your life to Jesus, Galatians 6:15.

- Circumcision is nothing. And uncircumcision is nothing. What is everything is when you obey God's commandments.
1 Corinthians 7:19

- Circumcision is nothing. And uncircumcision is nothing. What is everything is when your faith moves you to work for God because of the love God has placed in your heart, Galatians 5:6.

A young woman reads the Bible out loud to her grandparents

Q47) He loved a girl-like ewe.

136 A47) He loved a girl-like ewe.

God sent the prophet Nathan to David, the king of Israel, to tell him about two men in a certain city. One was rich, and the other was poor. The rich man had a very large herd of animals, many cattle, oxen, goats, and sheep. But the poor man had nothing but a little ewe lamb.
2 Samuel 12:1-7

A ewe is a female sheep.

The poor man let the little ewe lamb live in his house. He raised her as one of his children, sharing his food with her and even letting her drink from his own cup. He cradled her in his arms and held her to his chest. The poor man loved that little ewe lamb as his own daughter.

He loved a girl-like ewe.

Then something happened.

A traveler came to visit the rich man. The rich man had to feed his guest, but he didn't want to kill one of his own sheep. So, the rich man took the poor man's little ewe lamb. He had it slaughtered and cooked, and fed it to the traveler.

When king David heard what the rich man did, he said to Nathan, "That man must die!" And Nathan said to David, "You are that man."

Are you wondering why Nathan said that to David? You can find out in 2 Samuel 11:1-27; 12:7-25.

The Light of the world is born in a stable

Q48) Two Jesus called the light of the world.

Q49) Are all cops bad?

A48) Two Jesus called the light of the world.

- Jesus called Himself the light of the world:

> I am the light of the world.
> Jesus, John 8:12; 9:5

- Jesus called Christians the light of the world:

> You are the light of the world.
> Matthew 5:14

A49) Are all cops bad?

On Friday, June 4th, 2021, a group of teenagers went swimming in a pond in Worcester, MA. They were heard crying out for help from the middle of the pond. Police were called. Five officers dived into the water. Two teenagers were rescued. One attempt was not successful.

Five officers were willing to risk losing their life to rescue those teens. They didn't ask them if they were fans of the police or hated the police.

One of the police officers gave his life. His name is Emmanuel Familia. He was 28 years old. He left behind his wife and his two children. Officer Familia died trying to save the life of someone's child.

No, all cops aren't bad.

(continued on page 142)

Very few cops are bad. Most cops are good people who want to serve and protect their neighbors. Cops are super heroes. They're different from us mere mortals. We can't comprehend their bravery. They put their body on the line, risking serious injury and death, to protect us from very bad people, so we can go about our life in peace and safety.

Police officers' families are always praying that they come home.

But evil forces are trying to turn people against the police. They don't want you to know that it was God who created government, and law enforcement, and the military.   Genesis 9:6; Deuteronomy 19:15-21; Daniel 2:20-21; Romans 13:1-7

Police officers represent God. They work for Him. Police officers are anointed by God. One of the consequences of removing the Bible from America's schools is that now we have people who are so ignorant, they think it's acceptable to put their hands on police officers. God said:

> Don't touch My anointed.
> God, Psalms 105:15

If a police officer treats some people differently, that's a very evil thing. Everyone should be angry about it and demand that something be done about it. But when you make people think all cops are bad, they'll be less likely to comply with police, which puts both them and the police in danger. You're supposed to obey the orders that police officers give you, and do what they tell you to do. You're not supposed to sass them or fight with them or disobey them. Says who? Says God.
Roman 13:1-5

If you fight with police officers, and in their response, they make a mistake, or engage in misconduct, yes, they must be held accountable. But you will also be held accountable – by God. He will be angry with you for fighting with His representatives.

When you fight with the police, you're fighting with God.

Q50) He parted the Red Sea.

144 A50) He parted the Red Sea.

Did you say Moses? God said to Moses, "Lift up your walking stick in one hand and stretch out your other hand over the sea and divide it," Exodus 14:16. The word "divide" is # 1234, which means to split in two. But look at this:

> That night, Moses stretched out his hand over the Red Sea.
> And God created a strong east wind to divide the sea.
> In the morning, the seabed was dry ground.
> Exodus 14:21

In that verse, the word "divide" is also # 1234, the same word God used when He told Moses to divide the sea. That word is used to say God divided the Red Sea in Nehemiah 9:11; Psalms 78:13, and Isaiah 63:12. And these verses also say God was the one who parted the Red Sea: Psalms 66:6; 74:13; 106:7-12; 136:11-14. In Exodus 15:1-21, Moses and the children of Israel sang a song of thankfulness and praise to God for dividing the sea to save them, and closing the sea to kill the Egyptians.

> Oh Lord, You used Your breath.
> You piled up the water of the Red Sea.
> You made it into walls on both sides.
> And You made a hardwood floor.
> It went right through the middle of the Red Sea.
> And we walked across on it.
> Exodus 15:8

Joshua said this to Israel after he led them into the Promised Land:

> You watched as the Lord your God dried up the Jordan river.
> He made it so you could cross right over it.
> The Lord your God did the same thing to the Red Sea.
> He dried it up and kept it dry.
> He waited until all of us were safely on the other side.
> Joshua 4:23

A man can't part a sea. The Bible is clear. God parted the Red Sea.

Moses anoints Joshua

Q51) When Moses died, God appointed Joshua to take over and lead Israel into the Promised Land. And before Joshua led them, something was said to him six times.

Moses said it to him once. God said it to him four times. And the people said it to him once. What did they say to Joshua?

Q52) Three who lived on Earth sinlessly.

148 A51) When Moses died, God appointed Joshua to take over and lead Israel into the Promised Land. And before Joshua led them, something was said to him six times.

Moses said it to him once. God said it to him four times. And the people said it to him once. What did they say to Joshua?

They said:
>   Be strong and courageous.

In Deuteronomy 31:7 Moses said it to Joshua. And then Moses died.
Deuteronomy 32:48-52; 34:1-8

God said it to Joshua in Deuteronomy 31:23.

In the first chapter of the book of Joshua, God spoke to Joshua just before he was to lead Israel into the Promised Land. And three times God said it to him, Joshua 1:6,7,9.

Then the people also said it to him, Joshua 1:18.

A52) Three who lived on Earth sinlessly.

• Jesus lived His entire life on Earth sinlessly. Jesus is eternally sinless, Jesus is God Himself, the Holy One.

> God's Holy Spirit will come to you, Mary,
> and the power of the Most High will rest upon you.
> That's why the Holy One who will be born through you
> will be called God's Son.
>   Gabriel, Luke 1:35

>   There is no sin in Jesus.
>   1 John 3:5

• Adam and Eve lived on Earth sinlessly. But then they became the first humans who sinned, Gen. 3:1-24. We can't live on Earth sinlessly because we inherited sinfulness from Adam, Rom. 5:12; 1 Cor. 15:1-58.

Joshua and the spies bring back grapes from the Promised Land

Q53) How many of each animal did Noah lead into the ark?　　**151**

Q54) God singled out a certain evil thing as the worst example of what people do when they turn away from Him. Romans 1:26-27 says, "God gave them up to vile affections." It's so evil that God said if people who practice it won't agree with Him that it's a sin, then He will give them over to that sin. God said He will cut them loose, let them go, abandon them – and turn away from *them.*

What is that evil thing that God feels so strongly about, those "vile affections," in Romans 1:26-27?

152 A53) How many of each animal did Noah lead into the ark?

Noah didn't lead any animals into the ark.

In Genesis 6:19, God commanded Moses to bring the animals into the ark and keep them alive. Then it says in Genesis 7:7 that Noah and his wife, and his sons and their wives, went into the ark.

Then, the next verses, Genesis 7:8-9,15, say the animals went in, two by two, male and female, to Noah, into the ark as God commanded Noah. Then God shut the door of the ark.
Genesis 7:16

God led the animals into the ark. A person can't make the males and females of all the animals of the world go into an ark. Only God can.

A54) God singled out a certain evil thing as the worst example of what people do when they turn away from Him. Romans 1:26 says, "God gave them up to vile affections." It's so evil that God said if people who practice it won't agree with Him that it's a sin, then He will give them over to that sin. God said He will cut them loose, let them go, abandon them – and turn away from *them.*

What is that evil thing that God is talking about in Romans 1:26, those "vile affections" that God feels so strongly about that He abandons people who practice them?

God is talking about homosexuality.

Peter uses his sword to cut off Malchus' ear

Q55) Fill in the blank, multiple choice.

If you try to live a holy life like Jesus did, you will _____ .
2 Timothy 3:12

    A) Be thrown a parade

    B) Have health and wealth

    C) Receive honorary degrees from the biggest universities

    D) Be persecuted

Q56) He lived by the sword.

156 A55) Fill in the blank.

If you try to live a holy life like Jesus did, you will _____ .
2 Timothy 3:12

Multiple choice.

    A) Be thrown a parade

    B) Have health and wealth

    C) Receive honorary degrees from the biggest universities.

    D) Be persecuted

The answer is D.

If you try to live a holy life like Jesus did, you will <u>be persecuted</u>
2 Timothy 3:12

The Greek word for persecution means you will be hunted down. People will hate you and do cruel things to you, John 15:18-21.

You're a Christian, and you're wondering why you're stuck with so many sociopaths in your life. Thank God for them. God puts Christians in a refining fire to reveal our sins to us, so we'll give up our sins and obey Him. God is teaching us how to love people like Jesus loves them. And He lets us suffer so we'll talk to Him and cry out to Him. If things went well for us, we would just continue on in our sin. Sometimes I lay in bed at night groaning. And I cry out to God, "Please! Please! Please!"

A56) He lived by the sword.

Did you say Peter? No. Jesus didn't say Peter lived by the sword. Jesus said that about the evil people who came with swords to arrest Him on false charges, Matthew 26:45-57. Peter used the sword to defend his Lord. It was Esau who lived by the sword, Genesis 27:40.

A Christian is killed at the Colosseum in Rome

Q57) Fill in the blank:

Ephesians 2:8-9 says we can only receive salvation through our genuine faith. And Romans 10:17 says we get genuine faith by _____ .

Q58) Can you believe in Jesus and not be saved?

160 A57) Fill in the blank:

Ephesians 2:8-9 says we can only receive salvation through our genuine faith. And Romans 10:17 says we get genuine faith by _____ .

Answer:

Romans 10:17 says we get genuine faith when we listen to someone teach us lessons from the Bible.

A58) Can you believe in Jesus and not be saved?

Yes, you can believe in Jesus and not be saved.

It says in John 2:23 that Jesus performed many miracles, and lots of people believed in Him when they saw the miracles. And the most famous verse in the Bible, John 3:16, says anyone who believes in Jesus will be saved.

When John 2:23 says the people who saw Jesus doing miracles believed in Him, the word "believed" is # 4100. And when John 3:16 says anyone who believes in Jesus will be saved, the word "believes" is also #4100.

Yes, the people in John 2:23, who saw Jesus do miracles, believed in Jesus. But guess what. The very next verse, John 2:24, says Jesus did not believe in them. When John 2:24 says Jesus did not believe in them, the word "believed" is also once again # 4100.

John 3:16 is talking about people who believe in Jesus in the right way, genuine believing. A lot of people "believe in Jesus" for the wrong reason. A lot of people think Jesus is just a man. They don't want to know that Jesus is the Lord, the One who is to be obeyed, over all.

If you believe in Jesus, but Jesus doesn't believe in you, then your belief in Him is not genuine, you're not saved, you're on your way to hell.

So, yes, you can believe in Jesus and not be saved.

People on a street corner listening to Bible lessons

Q59) Can a goat go to Heaven?

164 A59) Can a goat go to Heaven?

Jesus said a goat *can't* go to Heaven. Goats go to hell, Matthew 25:41,46. When Judgment Day comes, the goats will finally have to face reality. There will be weeping, and gnashing of teeth, Matthew 25:30.

But *the* goat can go to Heaven. How? By becoming a sheep, Jn. 10:27-28. You do that by giving your life to Jesus and studying the Bible like you studied football plays. Then start throwing Bible lessons to people with the same enthusiasm that you threw the football (ooh, good one).

You did good. You took care of your family. You did your job. But you went too far. You didn't do anything for Jesus.

> If you win every trophy in the world,
> but lose your soul,
> where does that leave you?
>   Jesus, Mark 8:36

Oh, that's right, you haven't decided yet. Well, please, don't put yourself out. All God did was take on a human body so He could be nailed to a cross for you. But go ahead and take your time deciding. Don't stress yourself over it. Have some more fun and laughs first. There's plenty of time

Jesus wants you to take *Him* too seriously, overdo it for Him like you did for football. There's another arena, more dangerous and more rewarding. It's the arena you enter when you follow Jesus. The only real satisfaction comes from fighting for Jesus, Eph. 6:11; 2 Tim. 2:3.

You were willing to give your life for football. It's time to be willing to die for Jesus. Then you'll store up trophies in Heaven. The trophies you acquired on earth will rust and fade away. Jesus said trophies in Heaven never fade away. They last forever, Matthew 6:19-21.

You put rings in the place of God. They were your god, your idol. Your rings are worthless garbage, profitless, vanity of vanities. Throw them in the trash. Take your heart off your rings and give it to Jesus. Eccl. 1:2.

Samson was a Nazarite. He killed a lion with his hands, Judges 14:5-6

Q60) On the night before He was crucified, Jesus prayed to the Heavenly Father, John 17:1-26. And five times during that prayer, Jesus prayed that His followers be something. Be what?

Q61) True or false. The Bible says this:

> Money is the root of all evil.

Q62) Could a woman take the vow of a Nazarite?

Q63) Who is the father of the Jews?

168 A60) On the night before He was crucified, Jesus prayed to the Heavenly Father, John 17:1-26. And five times during that prayer, Jesus prayed that His followers be something. Be what?

In that one prayer, those 26 verses, in John 17:1-26, Jesus prayed five times that His followers be one. Once in John 17:11. Twice in John 17:21. And once each in John 17:22 and John 17:23.

A61) True or false. The Bible says this:

> Money is the root of all evil.

No, the Bible does *not* say money is the root cause of all evil. The Bible says the LOVE of money is ONE OF the root causes of all kinds of evils. It's not money, but the love of money – covetousness, greed, the desire to get rich, that is one of the root causes of many evils.

1 Timothy 6:8-11

The freedom to work and enjoy what you earn with contentment is a blessing from God, Ecclesiastes 5:18-20.

A62) Could a woman take the vow of a Nazarite?

Numbers 6:1-8 says both men and women could take the Nazarite vow.

A63) Who is the father of the Jews?

Jesus was speaking with Jews, John 8:52, and He said to them:

> Your father Abraham rejoiced to see My day:
> and he saw it and was glad.
> Jesus, John 8:56 (KJV)

Abraham was called a Hebrew, Genesis 14:13. He had a grandson named Jacob. God changed Jacob's name to Israel, Genesis 32:24-32, and his family became the Israelites. By the time Jesus walked the earth, they were called Jews.

Gnashing of teeth

Q64) He was the first apostle.

Q65) Fill in the blank:

> Husbands, love your wife like Jesus loves the Church.
> Jesus gave His life for her, so He could save her
> and cleanse her by the washing of water, with _____.
> Ephesians 5:25-26

Q66) Two instances of gnashing of teeth.

Gnashing means grinding or biting the teeth in pain or anger.

172 A64) He was the first apostle.

Jesus was the first apostle.

> Therefore my brothers and sisters,
> fellow-partakers of the Heavenly calling,
> who've been set apart by God to holiness,
> fix your mind on Jesus Christ,
> the Apostle and High Priest of our Faith.
> Hebrews 3:1

A65) Fill in the blank:

> Husbands, love your wives like Jesus loves the Church.
> He gave His life for her, so He could save her
> and cleanse her by the washing of water with the Word.
> Ephesians 5:25-26

A66) Two instances of gnashing of teeth.

Gnashing means grinding or biting the teeth in pain or anger.

One) Jesus repeatedly warned that the people who go to hell will weep, and gnash their teeth, Matthew 13:50; 22:13; 24:51.

Two) A good Christian named Stephen boldly taught the truth from the Bible. That made some evil men angry. They gnashed on Stephen with their teeth. Then they grabbed him, and took him off and killed him.
Acts 7:54

Jesus, the first Apostle

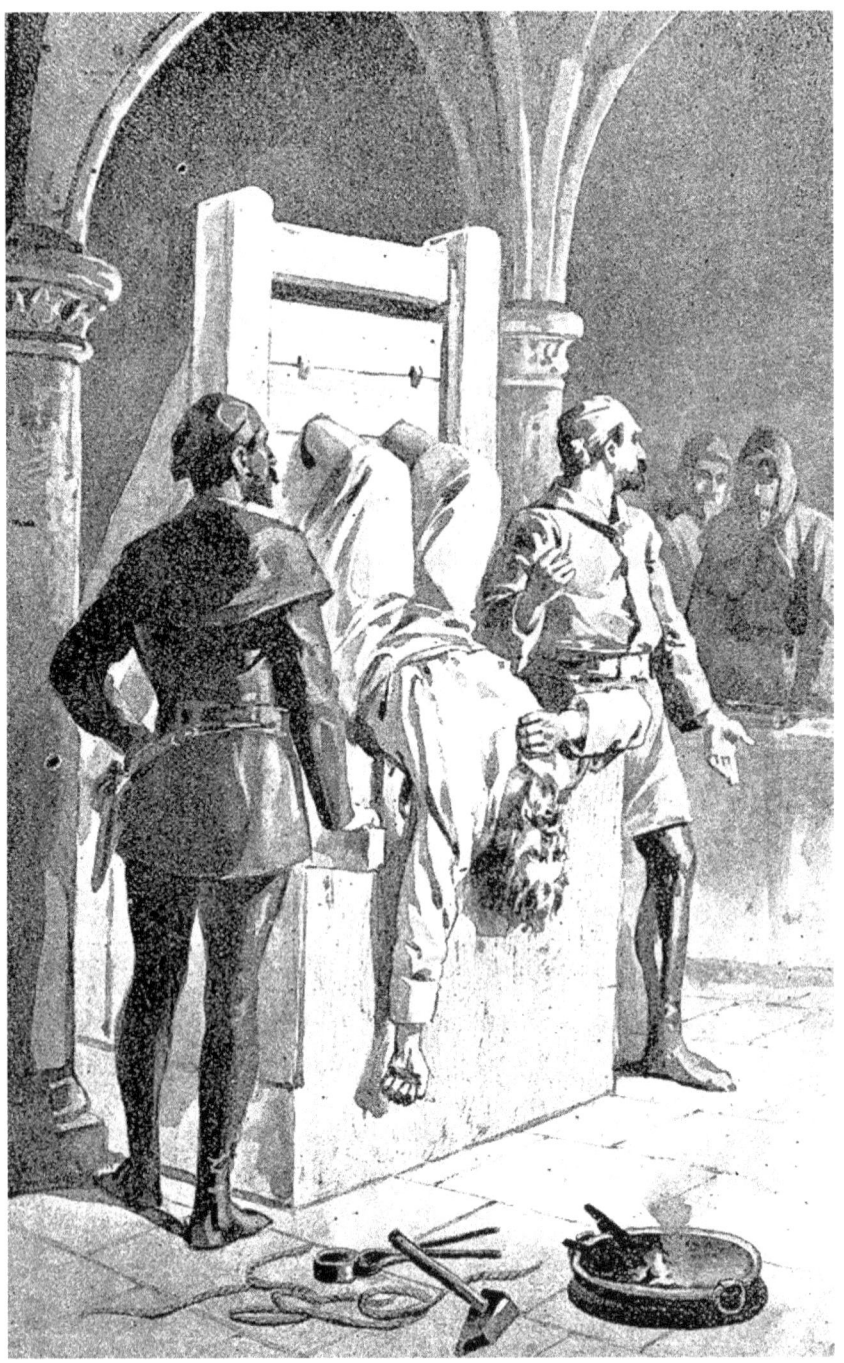

A Christian does four things to those who torture him like this

Q67) Is there a woman named Lilith in the Bible? **175**

Q68) In Matthew 5:44, Jesus commands us to do four things to those who do these four things to us: try to harm us, hunt us down, wish we were dead, tell lies about us. What are the four things Jesus commands us to do to people who do those things to us?

176 A67) Is there a woman named Lilith in the Bible?

No, there's no woman named Lilith in the Bible. She's mythological. But the word *lilith* does appear in Isaiah 34:14. The Hebrew dictionary in the Strong's says it means a screech owl, or night spectre, which is something like a scary ghost. It's # 3917.

A68) In Matthew 5:44, Jesus commands us to do four things to those who do these four things to us: try to harm us, hunt us down, wish we were dead, tell lies about us. What are the four things Jesus commands us to do to people who do those things to us?

1) Show a dutiful love to those who want to harm us

2) Pray for those who hunt us down

3) Speak well of those who wish we were dead

4) Do good to those who tell lies about us

Jesus is talking about our personal interactions with people. He doesn't want us to seek revenge or retaliate. He wants us to be patient and forgiving. He wants us to respond with love, not vengeance. He wants us to pray that they be saved if they're not.

Jesus is not forbidding lawful self-defense, Exodus 22:2. He's not forbidding seeking help from law enforcement, and using courts of law when necessary. And Jesus wants the military and law enforcement to make arrests, fight wars, and use deadly force when necessary.

Jesus told the apostles:

> Buy a sword.
> And if you don't have enough money to buy one,
> then sell your coat to get the money.
> Jesus, Luke 22:36

The sword wasn't for dicing vegetables. It was for lawful self-defense.

The mythological woman named Lilith is not in the Bible

The King of Kings is born in a stable

Q69) He said people don't live by bread alone (food alone). **179**

Q70) In which book of the Bible do we read about the revelation of Jesus Christ as King of Kings and Lord of Lords?

180 A69) He said people don't live by bread alone (food alone).

Did you say Jesus? Actually, Jesus was quoting someone.

Jesus was brought to the desert by God's Holy Spirit to be tested by the devil. Jesus let Himself be subjected to that testing so He could teach us by His example how to resist the devil's temptations. Before the testing began, Jesus stayed in the desert for forty days and forty nights, and He ate nothing the whole time. So, Jesus was hungry, Matthew 4:1-2.

Then the devil appeared, and said, "If You really are the Son of God, as You allege, then why starve? Here's some rocks. Turn them into bread and eat," Matthew 4:3.

Jesus replied, "It is written in the Bible, 'You weren't put on Earth just so you could eat food to give life to your physical body. You were given the precious gift of human life so you could eat every word that came from God's mouth, so you can give life to your eternal spiritual body,'"

Or as the King James Version says, "Man does not live by bread alone, but by every word that proceedeth out of the mouth of God."
Matthew 4:4

Jesus did not make up that saying on the spot. He was quoting Deuteronomy 8:3.

That's where God told the children of Israel why He fed them with manna during their forty year trek through the wilderness. God said He did it to let them be hungry, and to humble them, so they would learn that people must not live just by eating food, but must also live by eating every word that comes from God's mouth.

A70) In which book of the Bible do we read about the revelation of Jesus Christ as King of Kings and Lord of Lords?

Revelation

See Revelation 19:11-16.

Q71) Two called blessed among women.

Q72) Is the soul immortal?

Immortal means it can't die.

184 A71) Two called blessed among women.

One) When God gave Israel's army the victory over the Canaanite army, Deborah and Barak sang a song. They praised God for giving them the victory. And they also sang about what Jael did to Sisera, the captain of the Canaanite army, Judges 4:11-24.

They sang, "Blessed among women is Jael," Judges 5:24.

Two) The angel Gabriel called Mary blessed among women because God chose her to be the mother of the Savior, Jesus Christ.
Luke 1:26-38

A72) Is the soul immortal?

Immortal means it can't die.

No, the soul is not immortal.

> Don't fear people.
> Yes, they can kill your body.
> But then there's nothing more they can do to you.
> Instead, fear God.
> He can kill both your body and your soul, in hell.
> Jesus, Matthew 10:28; Luke 12:4-5

The only way your soul will never die is if Jesus saves your soul.

> God loves all of us so much
> that He sacrificed His one-and-only Son, Jesus,
> so that anyone who puts their trust in Jesus,
> will not perish, but will live forever.
> John 3:16

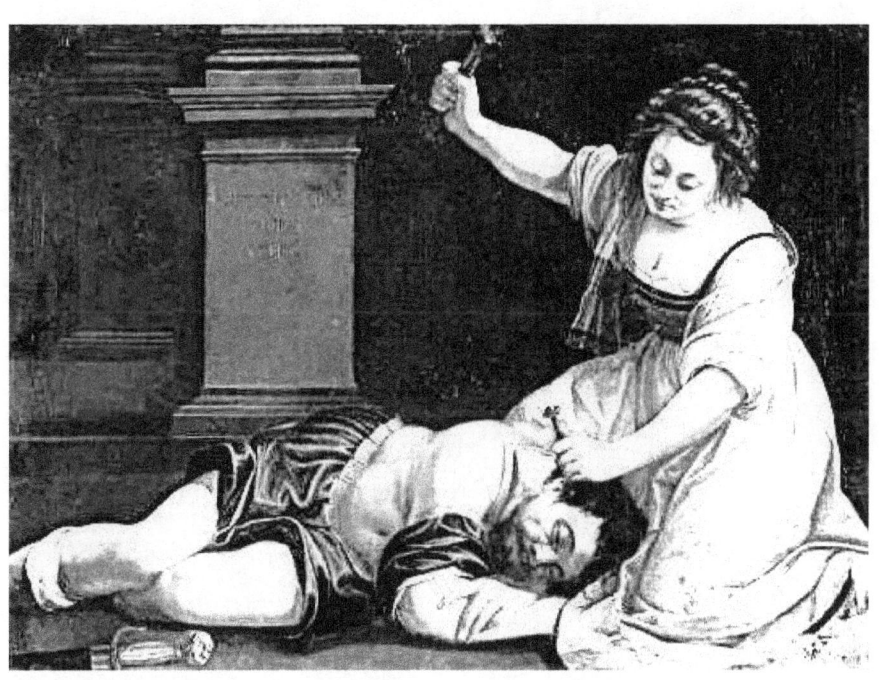

Jael does a righteous act

Q73) There's no less than 11 times when we read of Jesus sitting at the right hand of God:

Psalms 110:1;
Matthew 22:44;
Mark 16:19; 14:62;
Ephesians 1:20; Colossians 3:1;
Hebrews 1:3,13; 8:1; 10:12; 12:2

But there's one time – and *only* one time – when we read of Jesus standing at the right hand of God. Why did Jesus stand that one time?

Q74) The four words written on the high priest's hat.

188 A73) There's no less than 11 times when we read of Jesus sitting at the right hand of God:

Psalms 110:1;
Matthew 22:44;
Mark 16:19; 14:62;
Ephesians 1:20; Colossians 3:1;
Hebrews 1:3,13; 8:1; 10:12; 12:2

But there's one time – and *only* one time – when we read of Jesus standing at the right hand of God. Why did Jesus stand that one time?

Answer:

A Christian named Stephen was speaking the truth boldly and publicly. Some people hated him. So, they took hold of Stephen. They told lies about him. They falsely accused him of a death penalty offense so they could kill him. Stephen responded to all of that by boldly speaking the truth to his accusers. That made them more angry, Acts 6:1-15; 7:1-54.

Stephen was filled with God's Holy Spirit. He looked up and saw the sky open. He could see into Heaven. He saw the glory of God.

And he saw Jesus standing at the right hand of God. Stephen told his accusers what he saw. They hated hearing it so much that they held their hands over their ears. And they went into a fit of rage. They took Stephen outside the city and stoned him to death, Acts 7:55-60.

A74) The four words written on the high priest's hat.

Holiness to the Lord.
Exodus 28:36-38

Q75) The two of the 12 apostles that the Bible says were executed.   **191**

Q76) Fill in the blank:

> Behold, the days will come, says the Lord God,
> when I will send a famine in the land.
> It won't be a famine of food, or a lack of water.
> It will be a famine of _____ .
> 			God, Amos 8:11

192 A75) The two of the 12 apostles that the Bible says were executed.

One) Jesus told Peter that he would be crucified, John 21:18-19.

Then Jesus said to Peter, "Follow Me."

Later on, Peter matter-of-factly mentioned his imminent crucifixion, in 2 Peter 1:13-15. In the KJV, Peter refers to it as his "decease." In the original Greek the word "decease" is # 1841, the word *exodos*.

Over 2000 years ago, the Old Testament was translated into Greek for the first time. That translation is called the Septuagint. And in it, the second book of the Bible is called Exodus. That's because it tells of the children of Israel's exodus, or going out from, slavery in Egypt.

Two) The apostle James was executed by Herod Agrippa I, Acts 12:1-2. James was the brother of the apostle John, Mark 3:13-19; Luke 6:12-13.

A76) Fill in the blank:

> Behold, the days will come, says the Lord God,
> when I will send a famine in the land.
> It won't be a famine of food or a lack of water.
> It will be a famine of <u>hearing the words of the Lord</u>.
> God, Amos 8:11

Q77) Two times the number 666 appears.

Q78) Who did God say this to:

> Do you know why I gave you
> your position of authority?
> It was so that because of you
> I could show My power.
> And show it in such a way
> that everyone in the world
> would hear what I did.
> God, Exodus 9:16

196 A77) Two times the number 666 appears.

One) In one year, 666 talents of gold came to king Solomon.

1 Kings 10:14

Two) Revelation 13:18 says 666 is the number of the beast.

A78) Who did God say this to:

> Do you know why I gave you
> your position of authority?
> It was so that because of you
> I could show My power.
> And show it in such a way
> that everyone in the world
> would hear what I did.
> God, Exodus 9:16

Did you say Moses?

No. God said that to Pharaoh, the king of Egypt.

Pharaoh kept hardening his heart against God, Exodus 4:21; 7:3,13, 14,22; 8:15,19,32; 9:7,12,34-35; 10:1,20,27; 11:10; 14:4,8. When it says God hardened Pharaoh's heart, that's a Hebrew idiom. It means God let Pharaoh harden his own heart. God doesn't force anyone to disobey Him. That's not how God operates. He's just and fair.

Deuteronomy 32:4

The people of Egypt and the rest of the world worshiped images of animals and nature, idols.

Pharaoh's disobedience provided God with the opportunity to perform great miracles, Exodus 7:15-25; 8:1-32; 9:1-35; 10:1-29; 11:1-10; 14:1-31.

The miracles had a purpose.

The Egyptians would see God's miracles, or hear about them, and they would know that He was the one true God, the living God, the Savior.
Exodus 15:14-16; Joshua 2:9-11;
Isaiah 43:11; Acts 4:12

The tenth miracle was the death of the firstborn.

Q79) Which of the 12 apostles was a thief?

202 A79) Which of the 12 apostles was a thief?

The apostle Judas Iscariot was a thief.

Jesus was friends with a man named Lazarus, and his sisters, Mary and Martha. But Lazarus got sick and died. And four days after Lazarus died, Jesus raised him from death, John 11:1-46,53.

Later on, Jesus took His apostles and went to visit Lazarus and his sisters at their home in the village of Bethany. And there was Lazarus, who had been dead, sitting at the table enjoying a meal, John 12:1-2.

Mary had a pound of a very precious, very rare, sweet-smelling oil, called spikenard. She anointed Jesus by rubbing the oil into His feet. Then she dried His feet with her hair. The whole house was filled with the sweet aroma of the oil. But someone wasn't happy about it. It was Judas Iscariot, one of Jesus' twelve apostles, the one who betrayed Him.

Judas spoke up and said, "That oil cost a year's wages. Why wasn't it sold so we could give the money to the poor?" But Judas didn't care about the poor. He only said that because he was a thief. Judas was the treasurer of their little group. They trusted him to hold their money. But Judas was stealing the money and spending it on himself.

John 12:3-6

Jesus responded to Judas' question. He said:

> Leave her alone.
> She saved that oil to prepare Me for My burial.
> You'll always have poor people.
> But won't always have Me.
>   Jesus, John 12:7-8

Q80) Who was the first liar?

206 A80) Who was the first liar?

The devil was the first liar, and he was in the Garden of Eden.
Ezekiel 28:11-19

Eve was the second person created by God, and the first woman. Eve had a conversation with the devil, Genesis 3:1-5. Yes, I know it says she spoke with the serpent. But Revelation 12:9 tells us who the serpent is.

> The old serpent is the devil, Satan.
> And he deceives (almost) everyone.
> Revelation 12:9

The devil asked Eve, "Did God say you can't eat from every tree in the Garden?" Eve said, "No, God said we can eat from every tree. But God said there's one tree we can't eat from, because if we eat from that tree, we will die." And the devil said, "You will not die die!" Genesis 3:4.

Eve told the truth. The devil lied. But while telling that lie, the devil accurately quoted one part of what God said. Eve didn't.

God told Adam that if he ate from the forbidden tree, he would die die, Genesis 2:17. But Eve told the devil that God said they will die. By not repeating the word die twice, she took away the emphasis that God placed on the death that would result from eating from the tree.

When the devil told Eve, "You will not die die," he was lying, and opposing God's Word. But the devil knew God's Word better than Eve. Many deceivers know the Bible better than many true Christians.

An interlinear Bible shows you the original Hebrew. You can see that it says die die. The Hebrew language repeats things like that to make them stronger. So, God told Adam that if he ate from the forbidden tree, he will die die – absolutely die. God made sure that Adam understood. But Adam ate anyway.

> The devil is a liar, and the father of lies.
> Jesus, John 8:44

Q81) Is there a Black Church and a White Church?

210 A81) Is there a Black Church and a White Church?

No. God hates that idea.

> Spirit is what God is.
> Those who worship God
> must worship Him in truly spiritual worship.
> Now is the time for the real Christians
> to worship the Father in true spiritual worship.
> They're the ones God is searching for.
> Jesus, John 4:23-24

The Christian Church is not the place for black causes or white causes. It's not the place for black culture or white culture, or black music or white music. Those things are not spiritual. Black and white are not spiritual. They're of this temporary world, the flesh, the five senses. When you become a Christian, you check your skin color at the door.

Jesus said God is a spiritual being. Spiritual is eternal, incorruptible. God wants spiritual worship. That's Bible study, chapter by chapter. These verses say Bible study is the way to be filled with God's Spirit:

> If you're into drinking spirits to intoxication, you'll derail.
> Instead, <u>fill yourself with God's Spirit</u>.
> Then you'll make melodies in your heart.
> And your conversations will be like sweet music.
> You'll sing psalms, hymns, and spiritual songs to the Lord.
> Ephesians 5:18-19

> <u>Give the words of Jesus a permanent home in your mind</u>.
> Absorb His wise teachings and warnings.
> They will burst forth from you, as though you're
> singing hymns, psalms, and spiritual songs.
> Sing the teachings of Jesus to each other in all grace.
> And sing in your hearts to God
> Colossians 3:16

(continued on page 212)

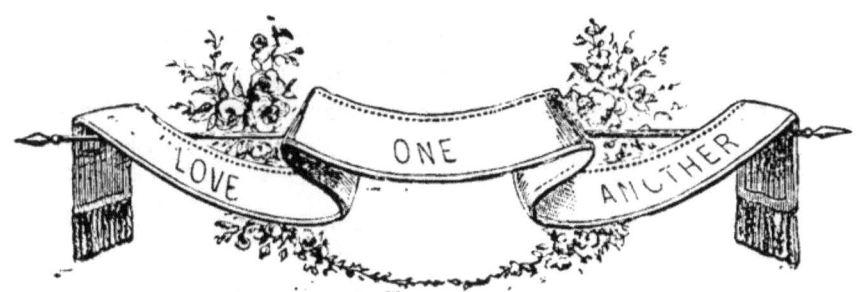

212 Christians have no black community or white community, no black theology or white theology, no Marxist oppressor class and victim class, Ephesians 4:1-6. We were all victims of sin who've been rescued and washed by Jesus, 1 Corinthians 6:9-11. We have no color and one mission – leading sinners to salvation through Jesus, Ezekiel 3:16-21.

There's no such thing as liberation theology. The societal injustice you're subjected to is not your cross. Your cross is the hatred you'll be subjected to if you become a Christian who teaches the Bible as it is.
John 15:18-21

Christians have real love for one another. It has nothing to do with the temporary things of this world, like skin color, race, or culture. We love our fellow Christians because Jesus loves them. We love them because Jesus commands us to love them. John 15:17. We sin if we don't.

We have a dutiful, sacrificial love for each other, as fellow soldiers of Jesus. We're commanded to see each other as better than ourselves, Philippians 2:3. Jesus said everyone will know we're His disciples if we love each other, John 13:35. The only way blacks and whites can love each other truly is if we receive Jesus as our Lord and Savior, so God can change our heart by giving us His Holy Spirit to live in us.
Romans 5:5; Galatians 5:22

Identifying as a black Christian or a white Christian is contrary to Christianity. It's a sinful thing to do. There's no place for pride over the flesh. A Christian's personal identity is irrelevant. Jesus told us to hate ourselves, Luke 14:26. We're commanded to focus on things above, Colossians 3:2. Christians are part of the Body of Christ, and Christ is neither black nor white. The color of your skin means nothing to God.

God doesn't see skin color. He only sees two kinds of people – those who want to obey Him, and those who don't, John 3:36; 14:21-24.

> The Lord doesn't see like people see.
> People look at the outward appearance.
> But God looks at the heart.
> 1 Samuel 16:7

Q82) The three things kept inside the Ark of the Covenant. **213**

__214__ A82) The three things kept inside the Ark of the Covenant.

1) A gold jar containing manna

2) The two stone slabs with the Ten Commandments

3) Aaron's walking stick that blossomed   Hebrews 9:4

What's that third one? Well, there was an incident. See, God appointed Moses and Aaron to lead Israel through the wilderness. But a man named Korah led a rebellion. Korah and his men accused Moses and Aaron. They said, "We're just as good as you. But you've made yourselves bosses over us," Numbers 16:1-3.

God needed to restore order. He had Moses tell Korah and his men to gather in one place. And God opened the earth under them. They were swallowed up. Then God closed the earth over them, Numbers 16:4-33.

Then God told Moses to have the leader of each of the twelve tribes of Israel take a walking stick and write their name on it. The tribe of Levi wrote the name Aaron, the high priest, on their walking stick. God told Moses to put all twelve sticks in the tabernacle. And God said He would meet with Moses there, Numbers 17:1-7.

God said the walking stick of the man He has chosen will blossom. Moses did as God said. The next day, he went to the tabernacle and brought out the twelve sticks and showed them to the people. All of them were the same, except for Aaron's. His walking stick had sprouted buds and grew flowers and almonds, Numbers 17:8-11. God did that miracle to remind the people that Moses and Aaron were the ones He put in charge, Exodus 3:1-22; 4:1-17.

So, the Ark of the Covenant held the Ten Commandments, which represents God's law. And the gold jar of manna, which represents Jesus. And Aaron's walking stick that bloomed, and produced flowers and almonds. What does it all mean? It means that when you revere God's law, and you love Jesus, then you'll blossom, you'll produce fruit. It means there will be evidence that you're genuine, John 15:1-11.

Q83) What mode of transport took poor Lazarus to Heaven?

218 A83) What mode of transport took poor Lazarus to Heaven?

Angels carried Lazarus to Heaven, Luke 16:22.

In Luke 16:19-31, Jesus told a story about two men. One was a wealthy man who lived the high life, eating and drinking merrily every day. The other man, named Lazarus, was penniless. He laid down at the rich man's gate, wishing he could eat crumbs that fell from the table. Lazarus' body was full of sores. Dogs licked them.

When Lazarus died, he was taken to the good side, where Abraham is. One day there will be a final judgment, when people will go to either Heaven or hell. But until then, people who die go to two different sides of a huge canyon. Abraham is associated with the good side because he received salvation through his faith in the sacrificial death of Jesus.
Galatians 3:6-9

When the rich man died, he didn't go to the good side. No, people don't go to hell because they were rich. The rich man in Jesus' story represents the fake religious leaders. Jesus told this story to condemn the fake religious leaders.

Jesus is condemning those who become pastors, and feast on the tithes of the people, while they neglect the people, and ignore their shabby spiritual condition.

There are many so-called churches and pastors who don't properly feed their people the Word of God. They starve the people. They don't care that the people aren't being fed the Word of God, and are dying spiritually because of it.

Q84) Who is the Queen of Heaven?

A84) Who is the Queen of Heaven?

This is who the Bible identifies as the Queen of Heaven:

> Can't you see what My people are doing?
> In the cities of Judah and in the streets of Jerusalem.
> Children gather wood so the fathers can make a fire.
> The women knead dough and make cakes on the fire.
> Then they offer those cakes to the queen of heaven.
> And they pour out drink offerings for gods and goddesses.
> They do that to provoke Me – to make Me angry.
>
> So, says the Lord God – Watch this!
> I will pour out My hot anger on that place.
> On the people, and on their creatures.
> And on the trees, and the food that grows.
> My anger will burn and it will not be quenched.
> God, Jeremiah 7:17-18,20

There are so-called churches all over the world today where people worship someone they call the Queen of Heaven. Don't believe them when they say they don't worship her. I've read their teachings. They speak of her in ways that the Bible speaks of Jesus. They put her in the place where only Jesus belongs.

They worship her as though she's God. That's idol worship. They're worshiping the devil. They've gotten billions of people to worship the devil. They claim she's Mary, the mother of Jesus. No, Mary is not the Queen of Heaven. You speak evil of Mary when you call her that.

There is no Queen of Heaven.

There is only the King of Heaven – the Lord and Savior, Jesus Christ.

This is the familiar depiction of a woman with her foot on a snake.

They put this woman in Jesus' place. It's Jesus who crushes the serpent's head. Jesus kills the devil, not this woman, Genesis 3:15

Q85) Four sets of twins. **225**

226 A85) Four sets of twins.

One) Jacob and Esau, Genesis 25:21-26.

The twin brothers, Jacob and Esau, reconcile, Genesis 33:1-20

228 Two) Zerah and Pharez

Judah was one of the twelve sons of Jacob (Israel). Judah sinned by taking a Canaanite woman, Genesis 38:1-2. God said the children of Israel must never marry Canaanites, Exodus 34:11-16.

Canaanites burned their children as a sacrifice to their god Molech, Leviticus 18:1-3,21,24-30; 20:1-5; Deuteronomy 12:29-31. They engaged in sexual immorality with no shame, Leviticus 18;1-30; 20:7-8,10-24,26. And they practiced the evil arts of divination, necromancy, witchcraft, and sorcery, Deuteronomy 18:9-13.

Judah had three sons with the Canaanite woman. One of his sons, named Er, married an Israelite woman, named Tamar. But Er was "wicked in the sight of the Lord; and the Lord slew him," Genesis 38:7 (KJV). Then, Judah's son Onan married Tamar, but Onan did evil, and God killed him too, Genesis, 38:8-10.

So, Tamar had no children. And Judah promised her that as soon as his youngest son Shelah was old enough, she could marry him. But when Shelah was all grown up, Judah forgot about his promise to Tamar.

Then Judah's Canaanite wife died. And Judah went to the city of Timnath to shear his sheep. When Tamar heard that Judah went there, she took off her widow's garments and went to Timnath. She sat by the side of the road with a veil covering her face, Genesis 38:11-14.

When Judah saw her, he assumed she was a prostitute. He didn't know she was Tamar, his daughter in law. He asked her to let him have sex with her, Genesis 38:15-16.

230 She asked what he would give her. Judah said he would give her one of his goats. But Tamar wanted something now, as security, that she could hold onto until he delivered the goat. Judah asked what she wanted. She told him to give her his signet ring, and his bracelets, and his walking stick, Genesis 38:16-18.

The signet ring identified Judah. It was a seal that was used to make an impression on legal documents. At that time, both Hebrew men and women wore bracelets, or armbands. Judah agreed to Tamar's request. He had sex with her and she became pregnant, Genesis 38:18.

Tamar went home and put away her veil, and dressed in her widow's garments again. Judah sent his friend with a goat for the prostitute, so he could get his signet ring and other items back from her. But his friend couldn't find her, Genesis 38:19-23.

232 Around three months later, Judah was told that his daughter in law, Tamar, became pregnant by engaging in sexual immorality. Judah said burn her, Genesis 38:24. He didn't mean burn her to death. The nation of Israel stoned people to death, Deuteronomy 22:13-24. Burning only took place after the stoning, as in the case of Achan, Joshua 7:25.

But Tamar had a message for Judah. She presented his signet, bracelets, and walking stick to him, and said, "Examine these closely, because they belong to the man who hired me as a prostitute and got me pregnant." Judah knew they were his. He said she was more righteous than him because he failed to let her marry his son Shelah.

Genesis 38:25-26

Tamar shows Judah his signet, staff, and armbands

234 Both Judah and Tamar sinned. But they were believers. Christians sin, Romans 7:14-25. But we have forgiveness because we belong to Jesus. So, God doesn't throw us away, Hebrews 13:5.

Look at what God did with Judah and Tamar:

Jesus, the Son of man, is a descendant of Judah, Genesis 49:9-12. Jesus is called the Lion of the tribe of Judah, Revelation 5:5.

Tamar is listed in the genealogy of Jesus, Matthew 1:3.

God forgave Judah and Tamar. God is so amazing, and so powerful. And He loves those who love Him, so much, that He makes good come from everything we do – even our sins, Romans 8:28. The good that God made from Judah and Tamar's sins was that Canaanites were kept out of the genealogy of Jesus.

Only Israelites could be in Jesus' genealogy.

Tamar gives birth to the twins, Zerah and Pharez, Genesis 38:27-30

236 Three) One of the twelve apostles of Jesus was named Thomas. The name Thomas comes from the Hebrew language, and it means a twin.

Thomas is also called Didymus, a Greek word that also means twin.
John 11:16

Thomas examines Jesus' wounds

238 Four) The apostle Paul was a Roman citizen. He was falsely accused of a crime. And he appealed to the Roman emperor Caesar.

Acts 25:7-12

Paul was put on a ship to be taken to Rome. That ship crashed. But all 276 souls on the ship survived, Acts 27:1-44.

Then Paul was put on another ship, which had for its figurehead, Castor and Pollux, the twin sons of Zeus, Acts 28:11.

The only person God buried when they died

Q86) I'm thinking of 3 scarlet strands.

One was when someone used a scarlet string. Another used a scarlet rope. The third was when a part of someone's body was compared to a scarlet ribbon.

Q87) The only person God Himself interred (buried).

242 A86) I'm thinking of 3 scarlet strands.

> One was when someone used a scarlet string. Another used a scarlet rope. The third was when a part of someone's body was compared to a scarlet ribbon.

One) When Tamar was about to give birth to her twins, Zerah put out his hand. So, the midwife put a scarlet string around his hand. And Zerah pulled his hand back in. Then his brother Pharez came out. Finally Zerah came out with the scarlet string around his hand.
Genesis 38:27-30

Two) Rahab helped the two Israelite spies escape from Jericho by using a scarlet rope to lower them out her window and down the city's wall. The spies told her God would send the Israelites to destroy her city. But they would spare her and her family because she helped them escape.

They told her to bring her family into her house and keep them there. And they told her to take the the scarlet rope she used to help them escape, and put it in her window, Joshua 2:12-21.

And they kept their promise. When they destroyed her city, they spared Rahab and everyone in her house, Joshua 6:16-17.

Three) In Song of Solomon 4:3, the Shepherd told the Shulamite that her lips were like a scarlet ribbon.

A87) The only person God Himself interred (buried).

When Moses died, God Himself buried Moses' body. And God never told anyone where He buried Moses' body, Deuteronomy 34:4-8.
See Jude 1:9

Rahab uses a scarlet rope to lower the spies out her window

Q88) Four times Jesus favored the right over the left.

246 A88) Four times Jesus favored the right over the left.

One) Jesus said that when Judgment Day comes, He will be in all His glory. All the holy angels will be with Him. Then Jesus will gather the people of all the nations before Him. And He will judge them by how they treated Christians.

He will separate the people one from another, like a shepherd separates the sheep from the goats. The sheep are the good people. The goats are the bad people. Jesus will have the sheep stand at His right. And He will tell the goats to stand at His left, Matthew 25:31-33.

Jesus will take the sheep with Him to Heaven, to live with Him there forever, Matthew 25:34.

And Jesus will tell the goats, "Get away from Me. You're condemned. Go into the unquenchable fire prepared for the devil and his angels."
Matthew 25:41

ST. MATTHEW. 47

ger, and took thee in: or naked, and | 43 I was a stranger, and you took me
 | not in: naked, and you clothed me not:

Jesus divides the sheep from the goats

248 Two) After Jesus rose from the dead, He stayed on earth for forty days before He went back to Heaven. One day, during those forty days, a group of His followers decided to go fishing.

They were the apostles Peter, Thomas, Nathanael, James and John, plus two other disciples, making a group of seven. They went to the Sea of Tiberias and fished all night, but they caught nothing, John 21:1-3.

In the morning, a man appeared on the shore. He called out to them and said, "Children, do you have anything to eat." They said, "No." The man said, "Cast your net on the right side of the boat and you'll catch some fish." So, they did as the man said. And they caught so many fish they could barely drag the net to shore. Then the apostle John knew who the man was.

He said to Peter, "It's the Lord," John 21:4-7.

250 Three) Jesus said if your right eye causes you to sin, then pluck it out and fling it away. And if your right hand causes you to sin, chop it off and throw it out, because destroying one part of your body now is better than getting your whole body destroyed later on, in hell.
Matthew 5:29-30

Do you think Jesus said something crazy? No, Jesus doesn't want us to pluck out our eye, or chop off our hand. He only said that to get our attention, to make us see that sin is a deadly seriousness matter.

And He used the right hand and eye rather than the left.

It's impossible for anyone to stop sinning. Every person will sin every day of their life. Christians sin, but it's impossible for us to go to hell. No, Christians don't have a license to sin. We're commanded to wage war on our old sinful nature. God provides a suit of armor. But we have to take the armor, put it on, and use it every day. And as time goes on, we'll sin less and less. Ephesians 6:10-18

> Listen to this, my beloved fellow Christians.
> God promised that He will live among us.
> Let's use that as motivation.
> We'll show God that we respect Him.
> That we believe Him.
> And we look forward to living with Him in Heaven.
> We'll do that by washing away every filthy thing.
> Let's aim for perfection – a life of holiness.
> The apostle Paul, 2 Corinthians 7:1

252 Four) After Jesus rose from the dead, He ascended into Heaven.

And Mark 16:19 (KJV) says Jesus sat on the right hand of God.

Q89) When was the final Passover? **255**

Q90) Three who groan in Romans chapter 8.

> In all three, the word "groan" comes from # 4727, the Greek word *stenazo*. It's when you groan from pain and distress, when things going on around you make you feel like the walls are closing in.

256 A89) When was the final Passover?

The final Passover was when the Lamb of God, Jesus, died on the cross.

> Christ, our Passover, was sacrificed for us.
> 1 Corinthians 5:7

We're taught in Hebrews 10:1-12, that the animal sacrifices in the Old Testament could never take away sin. So, they had to be repeated over and over. But the sacrifice of Jesus only had to happen once, never needing to be repeated. The one sacrifice of Jesus removes the ultimate punishment for the believer's sin.

A90) Three who groan in Romans chapter 8.

> In all three, the word "groan" comes from # 4727, the Greek word *stenazo*. It's when you groan from pain and distress, when things going on around you make you feel like the walls are closing in.

One) The Earth and all creation groans together, waiting for God to renew the Earth back to its sinless condition, Romans 8:22.

Two) Christians groan, waiting for God to free us from our corruptible flesh body, and put us in our eternal sinless spiritual body.
Romans 8:23

Three) God's Holy Spirit groans, making intercession for Christians according to God's will, Romans 8:26.

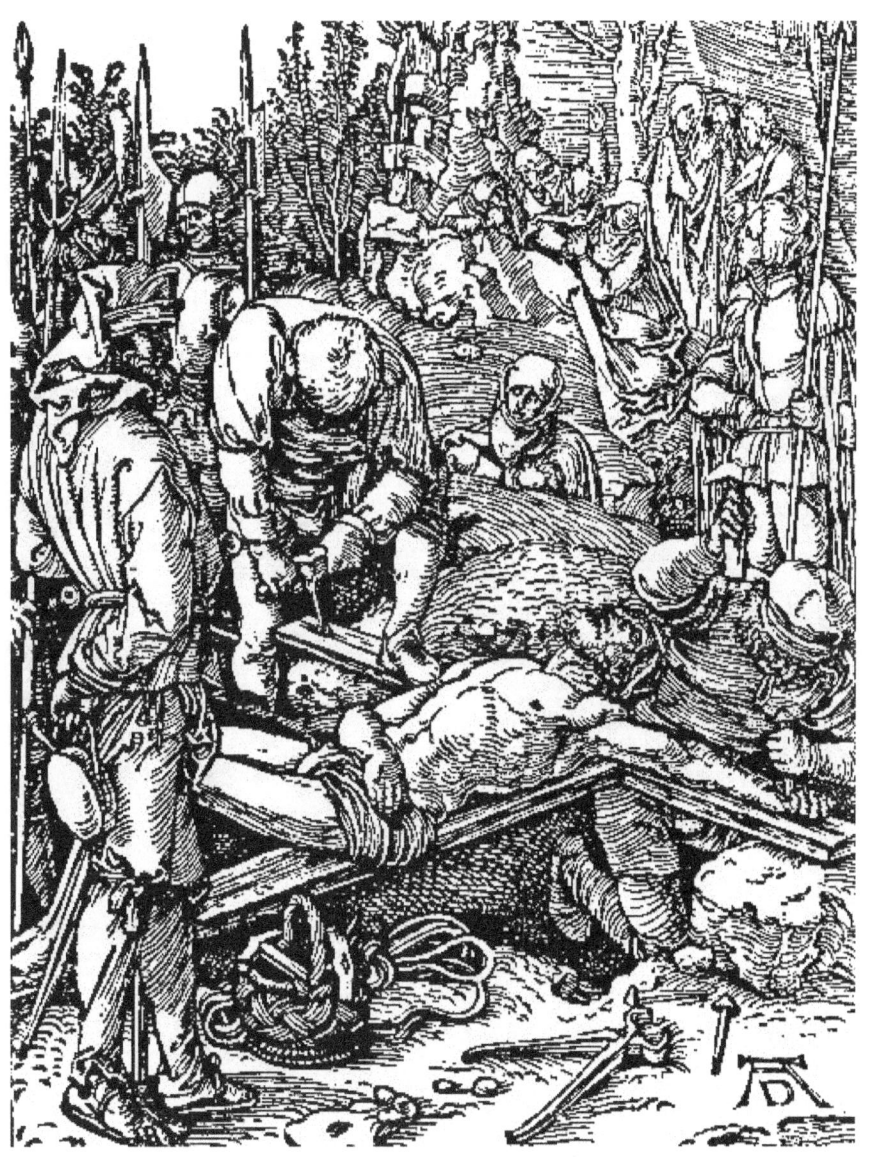

The final Passover

Q91) Two times Jesus wears a crown.   **259**

Q92) What does it mean when a nation needs to borrow money from other nations?

260 A91) Two times Jesus wears a crown.

- In humiliation.

Just before Jesus was crucified, He was brought before Pontius Pilate, the Roman governor, to be questioned. Pilate asked Jesus, "Are You the King of the Jews?" And Jesus said, "Absolutely!"   Mark 15:1-2

Because Jesus said that, the Roman soldiers stripped Him, and put a scarlet robe on Him as a royal robe. They put a reed in His right hand as a royal scepter. They mocked Him by bowing their knee to Him, and saying, "Hail King of the Jews." Then they spit on Him. They took the reed from Him and hit Him on the head with it. They took the scarlet robe off Him and put His own robe back on Him. Then they led Him away and crucified Him, Matthew 27:27-31.

There was one other thing they did when they mocked Jesus. They took some branches from a thorn bush. They twisted the thorns to shape them like a crown. Then they shoved the crown into His head.
Matthew 27:29

- In glory.

The apostle John was given a look into Heaven. He saw future events. He saw Jesus wearing a golden crown, Revelation 14:14. When Jesus returns to Earth, He will be riding a white horse. The armies of Heaven will be with Him, riding white horses and dressed in fine linen. And Jesus will be wearing many royal crowns, Revelation 19:11-16.

A92) What does it mean when a nation needs to borrow money from other nations?

In Deuteronomy 15:5-6, God told the nation of Israel that if they listen carefully to Him, and preserve and obey His laws, then they will loan to many nations, but they will never need to borrow from anyone.

That same principle applies to all nations. If a nation needs to borrow money from other nations, it means they've rejected God's laws.

Q93) Who does God whip?

Q94) Five-word statement made 3 times in James 2:14-26.

264 A93) Who does God whip?

> The Lord chastens those He loves.
> He scourges every child that He receives.
> Hebrews 12:6

The word "scourges" is # 3146 in the Strong's Concordance. It means to tie someone to a pole and whip them. It's the same Greek word used in John 19:1, where it says Pilate had Jesus scourged. So, the chastening God puts Christians through is very painful.

God corrects and trains His children. He punishes Christians for the same reason a loving father punishes his children. Because He loves us. When we're going through it, we might think – this is not fun. It hurts. But the painful experiences a Christian goes through have been carefully designed by our Heavenly Father for our good.

God puts Christians through a painful cleansing process. And as time goes on, we see that God used those times of trouble to reveal to us that we're still harboring certain sins. We understand that God is using pain to cleanse us of sin. And we try harder to resist those sins. We have a new stronger desire to obey God. Pain keeps us closer to God. It makes us cry out to Him in a way we wouldn't have without the pain.
Hebrews 12:5-14

And remember, Christians will not experience the ultimate punishment for sin. In other words – we can't go to hell. Jesus made that impossible. Jesus removed that punishment from us by paying for our sins when He was whipped by Roman soldiers and nailed to a cross to die.

A94) Five word statement made three times in James 2:14-26.

> Faith without works is dead
> James 2:17,20,26

John the Baptist shows the evidence of his faith by his works – by teaching the Bible and leading people to repentance, Matthew 3:1-6

Q95) Why I love to see women cry. **267**

Q96) He's called Holy Father.

Q97) His name is Reverend.

A95) Why I love to see women cry.

When I see a woman cry, it gets to me. It makes me laugh and cry. That's because I imagine she's crying over her sins and turning to Jesus. I cry because a crying woman is beautiful, because she's been humbled. Don't try to find beauty in lotions. The # 1 beauty secret is humility.

I can tell you in no uncertain terms that the most beautiful thing I've ever seen is a humble woman, and I've seen Larry Bird play basketball.

A96) He's called Holy Father.

On the night before He was crucified, Jesus prayed to God. And Jesus addressed God as Holy Father, John 17:11.

The name Holy Father belongs only to God. It's an offense against God to call a man Holy Father.

Jesus said:

> Don't call any man on earth your father.
> Because there is only one who is your Father.
> And He is in Heaven
> Jesus, Matthew 23:9

A97) His name is Reverend.

> Holy and Reverend is God's name.
> Psalms 111:9

The word Reverend refers to someone who is to be revered. It means you have a deep feeling of awe and holy fear for them. You have the highest love and devotion for them. Don't call a man Reverend.

Only God is to be called Reverend. It's His Name, and His alone.

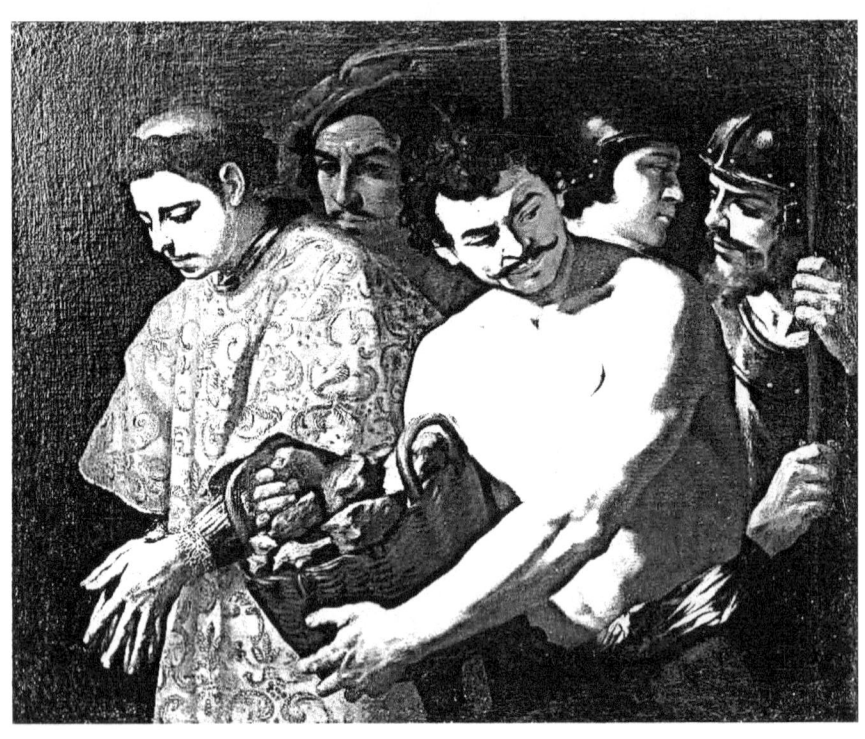

Q98) He had the face of an angel. 271

Q99) Two times Jesus hates.

272 A98) He had the face of an angel.

A good Christian man named Stephen was boldly and publicly teaching people about Jesus. The religious leaders hated him for that. So, they got some worthless men to give false testimony against him.

They grabbed hold of Stephen, dragged him to their meeting place, and stood him before them. They fixed their eyes on him, and looked closely at him. And they saw something. Stephen's face looked like it could be the face of an angel, Acts 6:15. Then they stoned him to death.
Acts 7:54-60

A99) Two times Jesus hates.

One) Jesus hates evil.

> God said to the Son (Jesus),
> "You are God, the King, forever.
> You bring justice to Your people.
> You love justice. And You <u>hate</u> evil.
> That's why God, Your God,
> has anointed You
> with the oil of overflowing joy.
> You have more joy than anyone."
> Hebrews 1:8-9

Two) Jesus said this to the Christians in Ephesus, and to all like them:

> There's something I really like about you.
> You hate what the Nicolaitanes are doing.
> I like that because I <u>hate</u> what they're doing too.
> Jesus, Revelation 2:6

Stephen is stoned to death

Q100) Two times Jesus tells people to eat Him.

276 A100) Two times Jesus tells people to eat Him.

One) On the night before He was to be crucified, Jesus met with His apostles for the last time, and they had a meal together. At one point during the meal, Jesus picked up some bread, blessed it, broke it into pieces, handed the pieces to the apostles, and said:

> Take, eat; this is My body.
> Jesus, Matthew 26:26 (KJV)

Two) Jesus said this to His disciples and a crowd of people:

> The living bread has come down from Heaven.
> It's Me. I am the living bread.
> Anyone who eats this bread will live forever.
> The bread that I give is My flesh.
> I offer My flesh to anyone in the world.
> To anyone who wants eternal life.
> Jesus, John 6:51

When Jesus said that, the skeptics in the crowd had an angry debate. They snarled, "How can this man give us His flesh to eat?"   John 6:52

Jesus said to them:

> Listen. I'm telling you the truth!
> If you show up at the door to Heaven,
> and you never ate the flesh of the Son of man,
> and didn't drink His blood,
> then you will not be permitted to enter.
> If you eat My flesh and drink My blood,
> then you will have eternal life.
> I'll raise you up at the end of this world.
> Because My flesh is the true food.
> And My blood is the true drink.
> Jesus, John 6:53-55

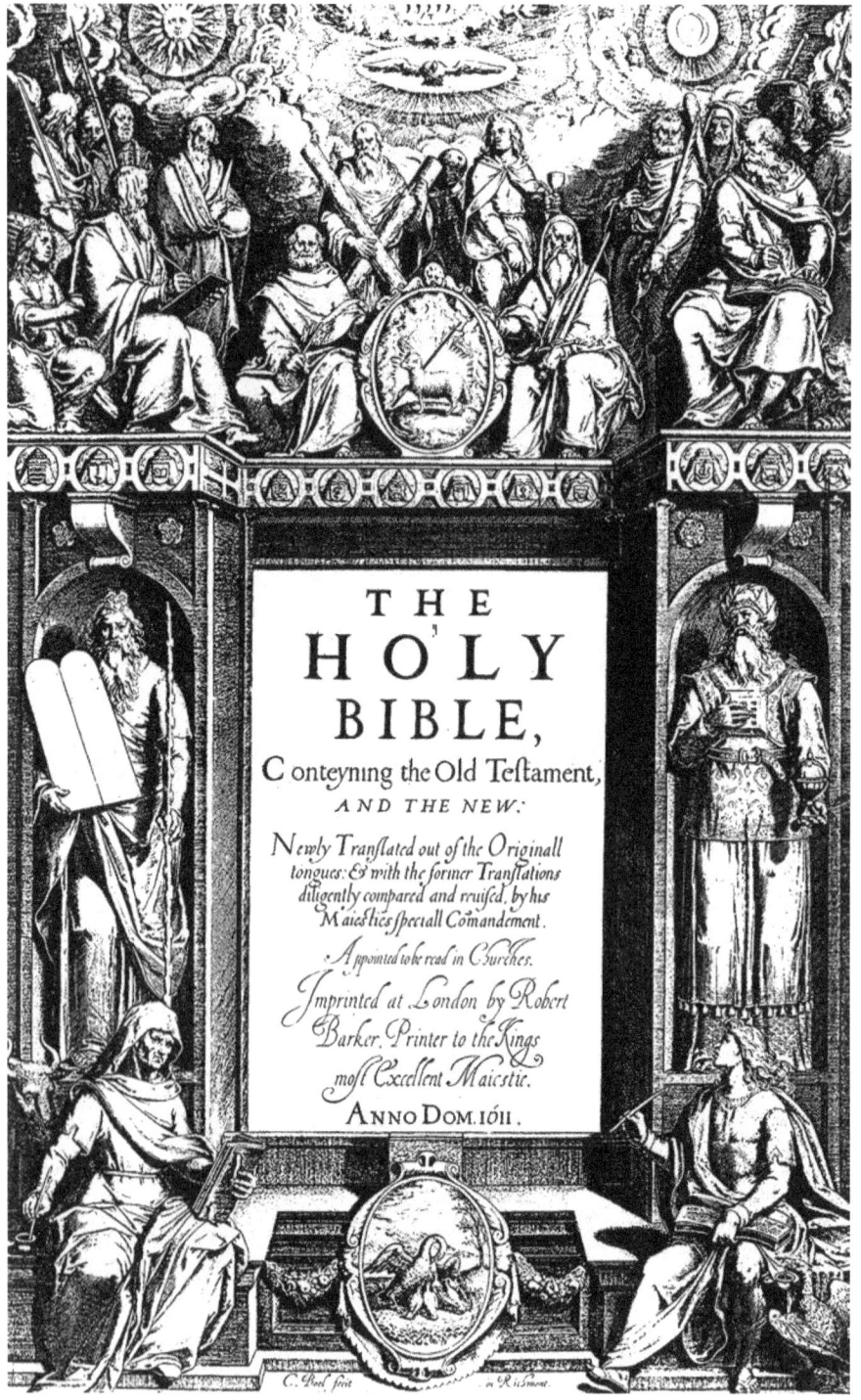

Q101) Three who got pleasure from eating God's Word. **279**

280 A101) Three who got pleasure from eating God's Word.

One) Ezekiel

God handed Ezekiel a rolled up piece of paper with writing on it, and told him to eat it. Ezekiel ate it and said it tasted sweet, like honey. Then God told Ezekiel to go and speak His words to Israel.
Ezekiel 3:1-4

Two) Jeremiah

> When You gave me Your words, I ate them.
> Your Word became the joy and gladness of my heart.
> Because I am called by Your name,
> Oh Lord God of Heaven's armies.
>   Jeremiah, Jeremiah 15:16

Three) The apostle John

Jesus showed the apostle John many things in a vision in the book of Revelation. One time, John heard a voice from Heaven telling him to take a little book that was open in the hands of an angel.

John asked the angel to give him the little book. The angel told him to take it and eat it up. John ate it up, and He said the taste of it in his mouth was sweet, like honey, Revelation 10:8-10.

Then the angel told John that he must teach many peoples and nations, and languages and kings, Revelation 10:11.

Ezekiel receives the scroll from God

Q102) I found three groups of people with different spiritual temperatures. How many can you find?

284 A102) I found three groups of people with different spiritual temperatures. How many can you find?

Burning hot, ice cold, and lukewarm.

One) After Jesus rose from the dead, He joined two of His disciples who were walking seven miles to a village called Emmaus. Jesus asked them what they were talking about. They said they were talking about a man named Jesus (They didn't know they were actually talking to Jesus because He hid His identity from them).

They said they thought Jesus was the one who would rescue Israel, but He died. Then, Jesus rebuked them. He taught them from the Old Testament why He came to earth, Luke 24:13-27.

Later on, the three of them had a meal together. Suddenly, Jesus took the bread, broke it into pieces, and gave the pieces to the two disciples. When He did that, He instantly opened their eyes. They knew He was Jesus. And as soon as they knew it was Him, Jesus disappeared.

The two disciples said to each other, "Oh how our hearts burned within us when He talked with us and explained the Scriptures to us while we were walking," Luke 24:28-32.

Two) Jesus told us that before He returns at the end of the world, the impostors who've infiltrated the Christian Church will give up the act. They'll show their hatred of Jesus. And the phony love they showed to real Christians will be laid bare for what it is – ice cold, Matthew 24:12.

Three) Jesus said this to the Christian church in the city of Laodicea:

> I've been watching you. Here's what I see.
> You're not hot. And you're not cold.
> I wish you were hot. Instead, you're lukewarm.
> Honestly, cold would be better than lukewarm.
> But because you're neither hot nor cold, but lukewarm,
> I want to puke you out of My mouth.
>   Jesus, Revelation 3:15-16

THE SUPPER AT EMMAUS

A cord of three strands is not quickly broken
Ecclesiastes 4:12

Q103) Why it's better to not be alone, according to Eccl. 4:9-12. **287**

Q104) After Jesus rose from the dead and went back to Heaven, His apostles did what He told them. They taught publicly about the salvation offered by Jesus. But the leaders of the religious establishment hated the apostles for doing that.

They took the apostles to their headquarters and told them to stop telling people about Jesus. Then they gave the apostles a severe beating, and let them go. As the apostles walked away, they rejoiced, Acts 5:41.

Why did the apostles rejoice?

A103) Why it's better to not be alone, according to Eccl. 4:9-12.

> Don't be alone.
> It's better to be with someone.
> Two together is beautiful.
> You'll make people happy when they see you two.
> And you'll get so much more out of life by having someone.
> When you fall, they'll lift you up.
> It's sad to say though what will happen if you're alone.
> You'll have no one to help you up when you fall.
> Besides that, how will you be warm when you lay down?
> If two lay down together, they will keep each other warm.
> Also, one person can be overpowered.
> But two together are much stronger.
> And a cord of three strands is not easily broken.
> Ecclesiastes 4:9-12

Suppose you're a husband and wife with no children. Who's your third strand? Make Jesus your third strand. It says in Psalms 37:23-24 that if you do that, then even though you'll still stumble from time to time, you'll never be utterly destroyed, because the Lord will hold you up with His hand.

A104) After Jesus rose from the dead and went back to Heaven, His apostles did what He told them. They taught publicly about the salvation offered by Jesus. But the leaders of the religious establishment hated the apostles for doing that.

> They took the apostles to their headquarters and told them to stop telling people about Jesus. Then they gave the apostles a severe beating, and let them go. As the apostles walked away, they rejoiced, Acts 5:41.
>
> Why did the apostles rejoice?

They rejoiced because God considered them worthy to suffer for Jesus.

Q105) Did Jesus sleep?

292 A105) Did Jesus sleep?

One day, Jesus sat in a boat near the shore of the sea of Galilee and gave a long teaching to a large group of people who sat along the shore.
Mark 4:1-34

When evening came, Jesus told His disciples to take Him to the other side of the sea. So they sent the people home and took Jesus into their boat and started sailing. But then a storm hit. The wind was too strong. The boat was filling up with water. While the disciples desperately tried to keep the boat afloat, Jesus was in the back of the boat, with His head on a pillow – fast asleep!
Mark 4:35-38

The disciples sat Jesus up and said, "Teacher! Don't you care that we're about to die?" When Jesus was fully awake, He rebuked the wind, and He said to the sea, "Silence. Don't move." And the wind stopped.

Then there was a great calm. And Jesus said to the disciples, "Why are you so fearful? Don't you trust Me?" Now the disciples were no longer afraid of the storm. Now they were terrified because they realized they were sitting in a boat with God, Mark 4:38-41.

The Old Testament says this about God:

> Oh, YHVH, God of Heaven's armies.
> There's no one like You, mighty Yah.
> You are the Faithful One.
> You rule the raging sea.
> When the waves arise, You calm them.
> Psalms 89:8-9

No one except God can tell the wind to stop and the sea to be calm. Jesus did those things. Therefore, Jesus is God. God Himself took on a human body so He could be the perfect sacrifice for our sin. He died in our place. But we have to receive Him, John 1:11-12. Jesus' human body felt tiredness, John 4:6. And He felt the pain of His crucifixion. If you give your life to Jesus, you'll be safe, even if you drown.

Q106) When God chose Moses to lead Israel out of slavery in Egypt, and into a land flowing with milk and honey, Moses tried to talk God out of choosing him.

Moses said, "I've never been able to speak well. It's like my mouth and tongue are working against me," Exodus 4:10-13.

God was angry with Moses for saying that. But God knows people have weaknesses. So, God said, "Your brother Aaron can speak well. If I have something to say to the people, I'll tell you, and you'll tell Aaron, and Aaron will say it to the people,"
Exodus 4:14-16

That doesn't mean Moses never spoke to the people. He did. And God was with him, Exodus 4:15.

My question is, if Aaron was the better speaker, then why did God choose Moses to lead Israel? I don't have a verse to document my answer. It's a conclusion I came to.

296 A106) When God chose Moses to lead Israel out of slavery in Egypt, and into a land flowing with milk and honey, Moses tried to talk God out of choosing him.

Moses said, "I've never been able to speak well. It's like my mouth and tongue are working against me," Exodus 4:10-13.

God was angry with Moses for saying that. But God knows people have weaknesses. So, God said, "Your brother Aaron can speak well. If I have something to say to the people, I'll tell you, and you'll tell Aaron, and Aaron will say it to the people,"
Exodus 4:14-16

That doesn't mean Moses never spoke to the people. He did. And God was with him, Exodus 4:15.

My question is, if Aaron was the better speaker, then why did God choose Moses to lead Israel? I don't have a verse to document my answer. It's a conclusion I came to.

Answer:

Even though Moses wasn't a good speaker, and his brother Aaron was, God chose Moses to lead Israel, because Moses didn't make a golden calf and tell Israel to worship it as though it was God, like Aaron did.
Exodus 32:1-6

Q107) Fill in the blank:

If you lack _____ , then ask God for it.
Go ahead, ask Him. He won't laugh at you.
God is a generous giver. He gives to anyone.
James 1:5

300 A107) Fill in the blank:

> If you lack <u>wisdom</u>, then ask God for it.
> Go ahead, ask Him. He won't laugh at you.
> God is a generous giver. He gives to anyone.
> James 1:5

In the original Greek, the word wisdom is *sophia*, number 4678 in the Greek dictionary in Strong's Concordance. You can't buy this wisdom. You can only have it if God gives it to you. It's spiritual intelligence. God can make you skilled in wisdom.

But you have to do your part. Don't ask God for wisdom if you don't study the Bible. Don't ask if you're not sincere. You'll get nothing.

God wants your whole heart. He only gives His Treasure to those who truly love Him, James 1:6-8.

Happy is the person who diligently waits at Wisdom's gates
Proverbs 8:34-35

Jesus' body is taken down from the cross

Q108) Who buried Jesus?

A108) Who buried Jesus?

When Jesus died, a man named Joseph of Arimathaea got permission from Pontius Pilate to bury Jesus' body. Joseph was a rich man, and he was a disciple of Jesus, Matthew 27:57-58.

Joseph was a member of the council that knowingly condemned innocent Jesus to death. But Joseph didn't go along with that decision. He was a good man who loved doing what was right. He hated evil. Joseph was looking forward to the day when Jesus would return and set up His righteous kingdom, Luke 23:50-51.

A man named Nicodemus brought 100 pounds of myrrh and aloes. Yes, that's the same Nicodemus who had a conversation with Jesus in John chapter 3. It says so in John 19:39. And women from Galilee who were disciples of Jesus brought spices and ointments, Luke 23:55-56.

Joseph and Nicodemus wrapped Jesus' body in clean linen cloth, with the 100 pounds of myrrh and aloes, John 19:39-40, as Mary Magdalene and Mary, the mother of Joses, watched, Matthew 27:61.

Joseph gave up his own tomb that he'd cut into rock, Matthew 27:60. That tomb was pristine. It had never been used, John 19:41. They put Jesus' body in that tomb and rolled a huge rock in front of the entrance.

Joseph's burial of Jesus is recorded in all four Gospels. It was the fulfillment of Old Testament prophecy. Hundreds of years before Jesus was born, Isaiah 53:9 said Jesus would be buried in a rich man's tomb.

Q109) What did God say you must *not* take satisfaction in? **307**

And, what did God say you *must* take satisfaction in? Jeremiah 9:23-24.

308 A109) What did God say you must *not* take satisfaction in?

And what did God say you *must* take satisfaction in? Jeremiah 9:23-24.

First, God said you must *not* take satisfaction in having the wisdom, strength, and riches of this world, Jeremiah 9:23.

Then, God said you *must* take satisfaction in understanding Him, and knowing that He is always willing to show kindness to anyone, and that He loves bringing about justice and goodness in the earth.
                                                                          Jeremiah 9:24

The ones who take satisfaction in the wisdom, strength, and riches of this world are satisfied with their own achievements, and with the temporary things of this world that will be destroyed.

The ones taking satisfaction in knowing God are acknowledging that the reason we know Him is because He gave us that knowledge. We give Him all the credit, and all the glory and praise.

Of course, we have to do our part. God gives the gift of knowing Him to those who diligently seek Him by being immersed in daily Bible study. I know I say that over and over. That's because the diagnosis is serious, and Bible study is the only cure.

If you only knew what you're missing.

A couple warms themselves while they read the Bible

Q110) Jesus called him the greatest person on Earth. **311**

Q111) One day, Jesus and His disciples were walking through a corn field. The disciples were hungry, so they picked ears of corn from the stalks, and ate the corn, Matthew 12:1

But what if they didn't own the field? And what if they didn't ask permission from the owner to eat the corn?

Would they be stealing the corn?

312 A110) Jesus called him the greatest person on Earth.

In Matthew 11:11, Jesus said John the Baptist was the greatest person on Earth. Jesus meant the greatest person other than Himself, of course.

A111) One day, Jesus and His disciples were walking through a corn field. The disciples were hungry, so they picked ears of corn from the stalks, and ate the corn, Matthew 12:1.

But what if they didn't own the field? And what if they didn't ask permission from the owner to eat the corn?

Would they be stealing the corn?

No, the disciples weren't stealing the corn.

What they did was legal according to the law of Israel. It says in Deuteronomy 23:24-25 that in Israel at that time, people could go into their neighbor's vineyard and eat all the grapes they needed to. But they weren't allowed to put any grapes in a container.

And they could go into the corn fields that belonged to their neighbors and eat their corn. But they couldn't put a sickle to the corn.

Can we go in our neighbor's field and eat their corn? No. That would be trespassing and theft, both unlawful. But the principle of those laws still applies, which is compassion for the hungry and needy.

John the Baptist, the greatest person on Earth, is beheaded

Q112) Over four hundred years before Jesus was born, the angel Gabriel went to a man in the Old Testament and told him when Jesus would be born.

Gabriel also went to a woman in the New Testament and told her when Jesus would be born.

Who were the man and the woman?

316 A112) Over four hundred years before Jesus was born, the angel Gabriel went to a man in the Old Testament and told him when Jesus would be born.

Gabriel also went to a woman in the New Testament and told her when Jesus would be born.

Who were the man and the woman?

One) The man was Daniel, Daniel 9:21-26.

ANNO TERTIO REGNI IOACHĪ REGIS IVDA

uenit nabugodonosor rex babylonis
in ierlem & obsedit eam : & tradidit dns
in manu eius ioachim regem iud ɫ & par
tem uasorum domus dī : & asportauit ea
in terrā sennaar in domum dī sui : & uasa
intulit in domum thesauri dī sui : Et ait
rex asphanaz preposito eunuchorum
ut introduceret de filiis isrɫ & de semine
regio & tyrannorum pueros in quib; nulla

318 Two) The woman was Mary, the mother of Jesus, Luke 1:26-38.

Q113) Three things Jesus said to take. **321**

322 A113) Three things Jesus said to take.

One) Jesus said this:

> If you want to go where I'm going,
> you must show Me that you're willing to
> go through what I'm going through.
> You do that by putting aside your old desires
> and by taking your own cross and carrying it.
> Jesus, Matthew 16:24

See Matthew 16:24-26

324 Two) Jesus said, Take My yoke upon you, Matthew 11:28-30.

326 Three) Jesus picked up a piece of bread. He dedicated it to God, broke it into pieces, and handed the pieces to His disciples.

Then Jesus said – take this bread and eat it, it is My body.

Matthew 26:26

Q114) Three times Jesus said "Me" when He meant His followers.   **329**

__330__ A114) Three times Jesus said "Me" when He meant His followers.

One) In Matthew 18:1-6, Jesus said His followers are like little children. And in verse 5, Jesus said if you receive My little child, you receive Me.

332 Two) In Matthew 25:40, Jesus said, "When you do good things for one of even the least of My brothers and sisters, you do them for Me."

Those good things Jesus spoke about in Matthew 25:34-40, include feeding the Bread of Life to hungry Christians by teaching them the Bible, Matthew 6:11. Satisfying their thirst for the righteousness of God, Matthew 5:6. Taking into fellowship those who are strangers to Christ, Ephesians 2:19; Colossians 1:21-23.

Clothing them with the righteousness of Christ, the garments of salvation, Psalms 132:9; Isaiah 61:10; Revelation 19:6-8. Sharing the Bible with those who are sick from practicing sin, and are imprisoned by the devil with the fear of death, Psalms 32:1-6; 2 Timothy 2:26.

When Jesus died on the cross, He took away the devil's power, Hebrews 2:14-15. Christians are forgiven for our sins. Jesus took our penalty by dying in our place, 1 Peter 3:18. We can't die in hell.
Revelation 20:6

The devil will be thrown out of Heaven by Michael and his angels, Revelation 12:7-9. Then the devil will be held by a chain in a pit for a thousand years, Revelation 20:1-2. Finally, the devil will be thrown into the lake of fire, where he'll die, and never be heard from again.
Ezekiel 28:18-19; Revelation 20:10

334 Three) A religious leader named Saul tried to destroy the Christian church. He imprisoned and beat Christians. He entered their houses and dragged them off to prison, Acts 8:1-4.

Saul hunted down Christians in foreign cities, Acts 26:9-11. And he approved of the killing of the Christian, Stephen, even holding the coats of his murderers while they killed him, Acts 22:19-20.

One day, Saul was on his way to Damascus to round up some Christians, when suddenly a light came from Heaven. Saul fell to the ground, and he heard a voice say, "Saul, Saul, why are you persecuting Me? Saul said, "Who are you, sir?"

And Jesus replied, "I am Jesus." Now Saul was shaking, he was so scared. He said to Jesus, "What do You want me to do?"   Acts 9:3-7

To be continued ...

Q115) Jesus said they're more blessed than His mother. **337**

338 A115) Jesus said they're more blessed than His mother.

A woman was listening to Jesus teach, and she said to Him, "Blessed is the woman who carried You in her womb and breastfed You."
Luke 11:27

Jesus replied to the woman by saying, "No, actually, blessed are those who listen to the Word of God and obey it," Luke 11:28.

Yes, it's a great blessing to be the mother of the Messiah. But an even better blessing is to be someone to whom God has given a love of Bible study, and who constantly agonizes to obey what God said.

Jesus wasn't saying His mother didn't study the Bible and wasn't striving to obey God. Always the Teacher, Jesus used the woman's statement as an opportunity to make a very important point. Actually, Mary was a serious student of the Bible. Here's how I know.

God sent the angel Gabriel to Mary, to tell her He'd chosen her to be the mother of the Savior, Jesus. And Mary said, "So be it," Luke 1:26-38. Then, as soon as Jesus was conceived in Mary's womb, she went to visit her cousin Elizabeth, who'd been carrying John the Baptist in her womb for the past six months, Luke 1:39-56.

When Mary walked into Elizabeth's house, John the Baptist leaped in Elizabeth's womb, and Elizabeth became filled with God's Holy Spirit. Those things happened because of the presence of Jesus in Mary's womb. Elizabeth boldly shouted out, "My cousin Mary – you have been greatly blessed by God. And blessed is the Child in your womb!"

Mary burst forth in praise to God. She said – God is great, and He is the One who has given me every blessing. And Mary taught Bible lessons. She praised God from the Scriptures, the Old Testament, Luke 1:46-55. Mary knew her Bible. She was a serious student of the Bible.

Mary was the mother of Jesus. And she was one of us who study, and take seriously what God said in the Bible, and travail to conquer sin.

Happy are those who listen to the Word of God, and obey God
Jesus, Luke 11:28

Q116) Who is God talking about in these verses? What did he do that pleased God so much?

> He deflected My anger away from the children of Israel. He stopped Me from destroying them in My zealous anger. He was as passionate for their well-being as I am.
> Watch carefully now and see what I'll do for him.
> Because of what he did for Me,
> I solemnly promise him eternal peace.
> I'm making him and his descendants My priests forever,
> because he was zealous for My honor,
> and because he pacified My anger toward Israel.
> God, Numbers 25:11-13

342   A116) Who is God talking about in these verses? What did he do that pleased God so much?

> He deflected My anger away from the children of Israel.
> He stopped Me from destroying them in My zealous anger.
> He was as passionate for their well-being as I am.
> Watch carefully now and see what I'll do for him.
> Because of what he did for Me,
> I solemnly promise him eternal peace.
> I'm making him and his descendants My priests forever,
> because he was zealous for My honor,
> and because he pacified My anger toward Israel.
> God, Numbers 25:11-13

Answer:

When the children of Israel were wandering through the wilderness, they made a stop at a place called, "The Meadow of the Acacia trees." That's where the Moabites invited Israel to worship their gods. And the children of Israel bowed down to the Moabite gods, and offered them sacrifices, and ate food in the temple of those gods, food that had been offered to those idol gods.

There were prostitutes in the temple of the Moabite gods. They had sex with men as a way to draw them into worshiping the Moabite gods. The men of Israel were having sex with those prostitutes. God was very angry about it. He told Moses to start executing the men who were having sex with the temple prostitutes, Numbers 25:1-5.

Moses and all the children of Israel saw an Israelite man taking a temple prostitute right into the Israelite camp. He took her into his tent.

Then, a man named Phinehas got a spear, and went into the man's tent. Phinehas saw the man having sex with the temple prostitute. So, he thrust the spear through the man and right through the woman's belly, Numbers 25:6-8. That's what Phinehas did that pleased God so much. Phinehas is the one God is talking about in Numbers 25:11-13.

Q117) Can humans eat angels' food, and angels eat humans' food? **345**

346 A117) Can humans eat angels' food, and angels eat humans' food?

Genesis 18:1-2 says Abraham was sitting in the door of his tent during the heat of the day, and he looked up and saw, "three men." It says in Genesis 18:1, that one of the men was the Lord God himself, YHVH.

Later on, in Genesis 18:16, we read that the three men rose up, and looked toward Sodom. And Abraham went part of the way with them. Then, the very first verse of the next chapter, Genesis 19:1, says two angels arrived in Sodom. Those angels were the two "men" who went to Abraham's house, with YHVH.

So, what did God and the two angels do at Abraham's place?

They had a meal. They ate bread made from flour, and freshly butchered meat that was prepared with butter and milk, Genesis 18:3-8.

So, angels can eat humans' food.

Sarah listens at the door while her husband Abraham, talks to God

348 It says in Psalms 78:23-25 that humans ate the food that angels eat. The first time we hear about this food is in Exodus chapter 16. It was at the beginning of Israel's wandering through the wilderness. God told them He would rain bread from Heaven for them.

He said they were to go out each day and only collect what they could eat for that day. God wanted to see if they would obey His law.
Exodus 16:1-5

The next day, when the people woke up, their visibility was limited because there was dew all over their encampment. But when the morning dew was gone, they saw that the ground was covered with small round things that looked like thinly sliced white frost.
Exodus 16:13-14

They didn't know what it was, so they called it, "manna," a Hebrew word that means, "What is it?" Exodus 16:15

It was the color of pearls and looked like small seeds. It tasted like wafers made with honey. They ground the manna on millstones, beat it in mortars, and baked it in pans. And it tasted like little pastries made with olive oil. God fed the children of Israel with manna for the entire forty years that they wandered in the wilderness.   Exodus 16:31;
Numbers 11:7-8; Joshua 5:12

Amnon rapes his half-sister

Q118) Three who had a coat of many colors.   **351**

352 A118) Three who had a coat of many colors.

One) Jacob made a coat of many colors for his son Joseph, Genesis 37:3. The word coat is # 3801. And many colors is # 6446.

354 Two) David's daughter, Tamar, had a coat of many colors. This is a different Tamar, not the one we read about in Genesis chapter 38.

This Tamar is in 2 Samuel 13:18. Her coat is # 3801. And many colors is # 6446. The same numbers as Joseph's coat.

Tamar was raped by her half-brother Amnon. Then, Tamar's full brother, Absalom, killed Amnon.

Absalom kills his half-brother Amnon for raping his full-sister Tamar

356   Three) After Israel defeated the Canaanite army, Deborah and Barak sang a song in which they praised God, and sang about the events of the battle, Judges 5:1-31.

They sang about the brave woman Jael, who hammered a tent peg through the brain of Sisera, the captain of the Canaanite army.
Judges 5:24-27

Then they imagined Sisera's mother looking out her window and wondering why Sisera was taking so long to come home.

They imagined her saying, "Did Sisera and his men divvy up the spoils of war? Did they each take an Israelite woman or two to have their way with? Did the men plunder dyed garments for my son Sisera and me, and did they find lots of embroidered dyed garments for themselves?"
Judges 5:28-30

The dyed garments are # 6648. Those are garments dyed with many colors. And the word embroidered is # 7553. It refers to garments that were embroidered with many colors. So, the people of Israel had garments, coats, of many colors.

Jael takes a mighty swing, and makes sure that Sisera can't steal Israel's coats of many colors. And, Jael makes sure that Sisera can't rape Israel's women.

Q119) Who are the only two who gave sight to someone who was blind? I'm talking about physical blindness. 359

360 A119) Who are the only two who gave sight to someone who was blind? I'm talking about physical blindness.

One) Jesus gave sight to many who were blind, Matthew 12:22-23; 15:29-31; 20:29-34; 21:14; Mark 8:22-26; 10:46-52; Luke 18:35-43.

You can read an interesting case in John 9:1-41.

Hundreds of years before Jesus was born, it was written in Isaiah 35:5, that people will know Jesus is the Savior, because He will give sight to blind people. Jesus said look at the evidence, Luke 7:18-23.

The apostle Peter told us God used Jesus' healing of the blind as a way to let people know that Jesus wasn't a fake, and to prove that He was the One, God Himself, the one and only true Savior, Acts 2:22.

362 Two) A zealous religious authority named Saul, thought he could serve God by killing Christians, Acts 22:20. One day, he was on his way to the city of Damascus to round up some Christians. But suddenly, a light came down from Heaven. Saul fell to the ground. Then he heard Jesus speak to him from Heaven. Jesus told Saul to get up and go to Damascus, and someone will tell him what to do, Acts 9:1-6.

But when Saul stood up, he was blind. He'd lost his sight. So, his companions had to lead him by the hand to Damascus. Saul didn't eat or drink anything for three days. Then, Jesus appeared in a vision to a Christian in Damascus, named Ananias. Jesus told him to go to the place where Saul was staying and restore Saul's sight, Acts 9:7-12.

Ananias did as Jesus said. He laid his hands on Saul, and he said, "Brother Saul, the Lord Jesus, who you met on your way here, has sent me so you can regain your sight and be filled with His Holy Spirit." Ananias put his hands on Saul, and instantly, things that looked like a fish's scales fell from Saul's eyes. And Saul could see.

Then Saul was baptized. He had something to eat, and his strength returned, Acts 9:17-19. Saul became the apostle Paul, a slave of Christ, and writer of Scripture, Romans 1:1.

But restoring sight was a sign that Jesus was the Messiah.

The healing of a blind person that God did through Ananias was a special, one-time-only event. Jesus healed many blind people. And He was born to a virgin. Jesus said He was God, many times, as He did in John 5:17-18; 8:58-59; 10:30-33. No sincere person would think Ananias was the Messiah rather than Jesus.

Q120) Three times one or more brought a coat to someone.

366 A120) Three times one or more brought a coat to someone.

One) When Jacob (Israel) made a coat of many colors for Joseph, his favorite of his twelve sons, Joseph's brothers saw that their father loved Joseph more than he loved them. It made them hate Joseph so much that they couldn't speak one kind word to him, Genesis 37:3-4.

One day, Joseph's brothers (except for Reuben, the oldest of the twelve) took Joseph's coat from him. And they sold Joseph to some slave traders. Then they killed a goat and dipped Joseph's coat in the goat's blood. They brought the coat to their father Jacob, and told him that Joseph had been killed by a wild animal, Genesis 37:13-36.

368   Two) A woman named Hannah was married to a man named Elkanah. Hannah was unable to have children because God put her womb out of commission. Hannah prayed, and told God that if He gave her a son, she would give that son to Him to serve Him. God answered her prayer. She gave birth to a son, and named him Samuel.
1 Samuel 1:1-20

Right after Samuel was weaned, and very young, Hannah took him to the House of the Lord, in Shiloh, and presented him to Eli, the high priest. She said, "I prayed for this child, and the Lord answered my prayer. Therefore, I'm loaning him to the Lord. And as long as he lives, he will be loaned to the Lord," 1 Samuel 1:21-28.

And Hannah prayed to the Lord, praising Him, 1 Samuel 2:1-10.

Samuel was a boy. But he served the Lord, and he wore a linen garment like the priests wore. Every year, Hannah made a little coat for Samuel. She would bring it to him when she and her husband went to offer the yearly sacrifice, 1 Samuel 2:18-19.

Three) The apostle Paul wrote a letter to Timothy, and asked him to bring him the coat he left with Carpus, in Troas, 2 Timothy 4:13.

Hannah loans her son Samuel to the Lord

Q121) Three who were handy with a hammer. **371**

372 A121) Three who were handy with a hammer.

One) One day, Jesus took His disciples to Nazareth, the town where He grew up. On the Sabbath day, Jesus went to the place of assembly to teach the people. But as they listened to Him teach, many of them were about to burst a blood vessel.

They said, "What kind of reasoning is He using? Where did He get it? And who gave Him the ability to do the miracles we've heard about? He's just a carpenter, for crying out loud!" They called Him a carpenter.

They took it as an insult that Jesus thought He could teach them.
Mark 6:1-3

Jesus responded by saying people appreciate having someone speak the Word of God to them – as long as they didn't grow up in the same house or town as them. Jesus was stunned by their unwillingness to believe in Him. He wasn't able to do mighty miracles there like He'd done in other cities. But He was able though to lay His hands on a few people and heal them of their illness, Mark 6:4-6.

Two) In Matthew's account of the same incident, he records the people as saying about Jesus, "Isn't this the carpenter's son?" Matthew 13:54-58 They called Joseph a carpenter.

Joseph wasn't the father of Jesus. God was. But Joseph was the husband of Mary. So, he was the legal guardian of Jesus when Jesus was a child.
Luke 3:23

<u>374</u>   Three) Jael proved to be handy with a hammer when she courageously hammered a tent peg through the head of Sisera, the captain of the Canaanite army, and fastened his head to the floor.

Judges 4:13-24; 5:24-30

The inscription is in Latin
It says, So may all Your enemies perish, Oh Lord

Q122) He only lived 365 years.

There was a man.

His father lived 962 years, the second longest life of anyone in the Bible.

His son lived 969 years, the longest life of anyone in the Bible.

But he only lived 365 years.

Who was he, and why did he only live 365 years?

378   A122) He only lived 365 years.

There was a man.

His father lived 962 years, the second longest life of anyone in the Bible.

His son lived 969 years, the longest life of anyone in the Bible.

But he only lived 365 years.

Who was he, and why did he only live 365 years?

He was Enoch.

Enoch's father, who lived the second longest, 962 years, was Jared, Genesis 5:15-20. And Enoch's son, who lived lived longer than anyone in the Bible, 969 years, was Methuselah, Genesis 5:21-27. Here's the reason Enoch only lived 365 years:

> When Enoch lived here on Earth, he walked with God.
> Then, one day, Enoch disappeared.
> That's because God took him.
>   Genesis 5:24

If Enoch was on Earth, how did he walk with God? The answer is in the New Testament. In his epistle, Jude reminded us that Enoch lived seven generations from Adam. And way back then, Enoch warned us about infiltrators, evil people who would sneak into the Christian Church by pretending to be Christians, Jude 1:14-15. That's one of the ways Enoch walked with God – warning us about fake Christians.

Jude said the evil people who infiltrate the Christian Church are the ones who pervert God's grace by turning it into a license to sin. They deny the Lordship of Jesus by making people think they don't need to obey Jesus, Jude 1:1-13,16-25.

(continued on page 380)

380   Enoch said Jesus will return with tens of thousands of His holy ones. Jesus will expose and punish all the evil ones for all the evil things they did in their evil way, and for all the cruel things those evil people said about Him, Jude 1:14-15.

We're taught in Hebrews chapter 11 that when Christians stay loyal to Jesus, through good times and hard times, that's the evidence that we truly believe God's promises. We're told in Hebrews chapter 11 about the excellent things believers did because of their faithfulness to Jesus.

Hebrews 11:5 says Enoch didn't have to experience death, and God took Enoch to Himself, because God was grateful for what Enoch did for Him. God enjoyed what Enoch did. God took satisfaction in the faithful work Enoch did for Him.

And God listed Enoch in the genealogy of Jesus in Luke 3:23-38 (v. 37).

Q123) Jesus divided the Old Testament into three parts. **381**

What are the three? Luke 24:44.

382 A123) Jesus divided the Old Testament into three parts.

>What are the three? Luke 24:44.

First, you need to know that Jesus told His disciples that He would die. Jesus told them that the Old Testament said He would die. But they didn't understand.

> Jesus took His twelve apostles aside, and said to them,
> "Listen carefully. We're going to Jerusalem.
> And everything will happen to the Son of man just as it
> was foretold by the prophets in the Old Testament.
> He will be handed over to unbelievers.
> They will taunt and torment Him, and spit on Him.
> Then they will whip Him, and kill Him.
> And three days later He will rise from death and live again."
> But the apostles didn't understand any of what Jesus said.
> Luke 18:31-34

In those verses, Jesus called Himself the Son of man, and referred to Himself in the third person, saying "He" and "Him" instead of "I."

After He rose from death, Jesus suddenly appeared to the apostles. When they saw Jesus, the apostles thought they were seeing a ghost. They were frozen in fear, Luke 24:33-43. And Jesus said this to His eleven apostles (Judas was dead):

> "I kept on telling you before
> about all the things that would happen to Me.
> And those things did happen.
> They completed what had been written about Me
> in the Law of Moses,
> and in the Prophets,
> and in the Psalms."
> Then Jesus opened their mind completely
> so they could understand the Bible.
> Luke 24:44-45

(continued on page 384)

After Jesus rose from the dead, He walked through a wall to surprise His apostles, who had locked themselves in a room

384 Did you see that? Jesus mentioned the three parts of the Hebrew Bible. The three parts were divided up like this:

- **The Law of Moses**: Genesis, Exodus, Leviticus, Numbers, Deuteronomy.

- **The Prophets**: Joshua, Judges, Samuel, Kings, Isaiah, Jeremiah, Ezekiel, the Minor Prophets.

- **The Psalms** (or the Writings): Ruth, Chronicles, Ezra-Nehemiah, Esther, Job, Psalms, Proverbs, Ecclesiastes, Song of Solomon, Lamentations, Daniel.

In Hebrew, The Law is Torah. The Prophets is Neviim. The Psalms is Ketuvim You'll see them abbreviated as TNK, or Tanach.

The disciples of Jesus eventually remembered what He told them about His death and resurrection, and they believed what the Old Testament said, and believed the words that Jesus spoke to them, John 2:22.

Q124) Four men who found a wife at a well (or was found for him). **385**

386 A124) Four men who found a wife at a well (or was found for him).

One) Abraham was living among people called Canaanites, who did not worship the one true God like Abraham did. Abraham didn't want his son Isaac to marry a Canaanite woman. So he sent his most senior servant on a mission to find a wife for Isaac in the country he'd left, the country where he was from, where his family lived.

Abraham's servant went there and found Rebekah at a well. She agreed to go with him. Rebekah became Isaac's wife, Genesis 24:1-67.

388 Two) Isaac and Rebekah had two sons, twins, named Jacob and Esau, Genesis 25:20-28. Esau came to hate Jacob and wanted to kill him.

So, Rebekah sent Jacob to live with her brother Laban, Genesis 27:41-46. When Jacob arrived in the land of Rebekah's family, he came to a well. He met a woman there, named Rachel. She would become his wife.
Genesis 29:1-28

390 Three) Jacob, who was now called Israel, moved his family to Egypt because of a famine. The king of Egypt blessed them, and the children of Israel prospered there. But then a new king took over in Egypt. That king was concerned that the Israelites were becoming too powerful. So, he enslaved them. He even commanded that all the male children born to the Israelites be killed, and only their daughters be allowed to live, Exodus 1:8-22.

An Israelite man named Amram and his wife Jochebed, lived in Egypt, Exodus 6:20. And Jochedbed gave birth to their son, Moses. They saw that Moses was beautiful to God, Acts 7:20. And they weren't afraid of the king. They hid Moses from the king for three months, Exodus 2:2. Because of that, God called them faithful, loyal people, Hebrews 11:23.

When Moses was three months old, his mother put him in a little boat and hid him among the reeds near the banks of the Nile river. And, Moses' sister Miriam kept watch over little Moses in the boat. Then the daughter of the king of Egypt came to the river to bathe and found Moses in the river, Exodus 2:3-6.

She adopted Moses as her own son, Exodus 2:10. And as the son of the king's daughter, Moses was taught all the wisdom of Egypt. His words and actions were weighty, Acts 7:22.

But one day, Moses witnessed an evil act of injustice. An Egyptian was beating an Israelite. Moses stepped in and physically defended the Israelite. Moses performed a righteous act of self-defense.
Exodus 2:11-12; Acts 7:23-24

But when Moses struck the Egyptian, the Egyptian died. When the king of Egypt heard that Moses killed an Egyptian, the king wanted to kill Moses. So, Moses fled Egypt and went to the land of Midian, and sat down beside a well, Exodus 2:15.

Then seven women came to the well, seven sisters, the daughters of one man, named Reuel. The women started drawing water for their flock. But some shepherds came and drove them away. So, Moses got up and helped the sisters.   (continued on page 392)

392 Moses even drew water for their flock. And when the women got home, their father asked them why they were home so early. They said an Egyptian rescued them from some shepherds, and even drew water for their flock (Moses was an Israelite, but they thought he was an Egyptian because he was still dressed like one).

Reuel told his daughters to go find the man who helped them and invite him to dinner. Then Moses moved in with them. And he married one of Reuel's daughters, named Zipporah, that he met at the well.

Exodus 2:16-21

The Marriage of Moses

__394__ Four) Jesus made a long walk to Jacob's well, in Samaria. There was a woman there that He wanted to lead to salvation. Jesus sat on the well and waited for her. It was around noontime.

Then she arrived and began drawing water. Jesus asked her to give Him a drink of water, John 4:1-8. She knew Jesus was Jewish because of the way He was dressed. So, she asked Him why He would request a drink of water from her, seeing Jews don't interact with Samaritans.
John 4:9; Acts 10:28; 11;1-3

Jesus ignored her question. He told her that if she'd known the Gift God wants to give her, and if she'd known who He was, then she would have asked *Him* for a drink of water, and He would have given her Living Water. She said, "Sir, where will You get this Living Water? The well is deep. And You don't have anything to draw the water."

Again, Jesus ignored her question, and said, "If you drink the water from the well, you'll get thirsty again. But whoever drinks the water I give, will never thirst. The water I give will be a well of water springing up in them, and will cause them to live forever." The woman said to Jesus "Sir, give me this water ... " John 4:10-15.

Jesus taught her that He was the Savior, John 4:16-26. She dropped her water pot and went to her city to tell the people there that she met the Savior. And many of those Samaritans committed their life to Jesus because of her testimony. Then many others came to Jesus Himself, and they believed in Him because of what He said to them.
John 4:28-30,39-42

That Samaritan woman became part of the Church, the wife of Christ:

> Husbands, learn from Jesus.
> He loves His wife, the Church, so much,
> that He gave His life for her.
> Love your wife that much.
> Ephesians 5:25

(continued on page 396)

396 The apostle Paul wrote this to the Church:

> I am indeed zealous for you, with the zeal of God.
> I've engaged you to one husband, namely Christ.
> And I promised to present you as a holy bride to Him.
> 2 Corinthians 11:2

Jesus is called the Lamb, John 1:29,36. And Revelation 19:7-9 talks about the Lamb's wife, and the marriage supper of the Lamb.

So, Jesus met a wife at a well, the Samaritan woman who received Him as her Lord and Savior, and who proved that her faith was genuine by her works, when she told her neighbors that she met the Savior.

Q125) Three times someone told Jesus not to do something. **397**

398 A125) Three times someone told Jesus not to do something.

One) John the Baptist was a prophet, which means he spoke for God. John lived in the wilderness. He was preaching, and telling people to repent of their sins. And many people came to him to undergo the symbolic act of water baptism in the Jordan river, Matthew 3:5-6.

Then Jesus came to John to be baptized. John refused. He tried to talk Jesus out of it. But Jesus told John to baptize Him so He can dot the i's and cross the t's. Then John baptized Jesus, Matthew 3:13-15.

Jesus never sinned. So, He didn't need to be baptized, and He didn't need to repent. He got baptized to humble Himself, as though He was just a man. Jesus did that to teach us that we must obey God.

__400__ Two) One day, Jesus was reminding His disciples that He will be killed and then rise from death after three days. And the apostle Peter took Jesus by the hand and started rebuking Him.

Peter said "Lord, let's get that weight off Your shoulders. That will never happen to You!"

Jesus turned to Peter and said, "Get behind Me Satan! You're trying to catch Me in your trap. You're thinking like a man instead of like God."

Matthew 16:21-23

402   Three) On the night before He was crucified, Jesus had one last meeting with His apostles. You can read about it in John, chs. 13 to 17. After they had supper, Jesus stood up, removed His outer garments, tied a towel around Himself, and poured water into a basin. Then, He began washing the apostles feet, and wiping their feet with the towel.

When it was Peter's turn to have his feet washed, Peter said to Jesus, "Lord, are You going to wash my feet?" Jesus said, "You don't know now why I'm doing this, but later on you'll understand." But Peter said, "No, You'll never wash my feet."

Jesus replied, "If I don't wash your feet, it means you have nothing to do with Me." And Peter said, "Lord, then don't just wash my feet, wash my hands and my head too."

Jesus said, "No, I've already washed you. You're completely clean now. You don't need Me to wash you again – except for your feet."
John 13:4-10

What Jesus meant is that He washed Peter completely when He gave him salvation. Jesus made Peter into a new person, 2 Corinthians 5:17. That's something that happens once, and never has to be done again.

But all Christians, including Peter, still have our old sinful nature living in our flesh body. And for as long as we walk through this world, we'll constantly be tempted by sinful things that come at us, Romans 7:14-25. So, that's why Jesus said we have to keep washing our feet.

Jesus keeps our feet clean. And we have to keep our feet clean. Really? Yes, it's Jesus and it's us. Another beautiful Biblical paradox.

>Wash yourselves and be holy,
>   Leviticus 20:7

>I am the Lord who washes you.
>   Leviticus 20:8

Q126) Three times something was written by the finger of God.   **405**

406 A126) Three times something was written by the finger of God.

One) Moses went up on Mount Sinai to meet with God. He waited while God used His finger to write the Ten Commandments on two stone slabs, Exodus 31:18.

Moses started down the mountain, carrying the two slabs. But he threw them to the ground and broke them to pieces. That's because he saw the children of Israel worshiping and celebrating around a golden calf that they'd made while he was gone. Exodus 32:19; Deuteronomy 9:8-21

So, God had to write the Ten Commandments again on two new stone slabs, Exodus 34:1-5, 28-35.

408 Two) The king of Babylon, Belshazzar, invited a thousand of his best people to a party, Daniel 5:1.

A while back, Belshazzar's grandfather, king Nebuchadnezzar, invaded Israel and looted the temple in Jerusalem. He took the holy cups made of gold and silver that were used to worship the one true living God. He brought those cups to Babylon and stashed them away.
2 Chronicles 36:9-21

God let Nebuchadnezzar do that, Isaiah 39:5-8. God loved Israel. But they left Him to worship idols. God chastises those He loves.
Hebrews 12:6

And now, at the party, Belshazzar had an idea. He commanded his servants to go and get those cups that Nebuchadnezzar took from God's house. Belshazzar and his guests drank wine from them. And, while they drank, they praised their gods, the dead idols they'd carved from metal, wood, and stone, Daniel 5:2-4.

Then something happened that wiped the smile from Belshazzar's face. He was terrified. He went ashen, his hip bone gave way, and his knees knocked. That's because he saw a hand writing on the wall. Belshazzar saw his demise written on the wall by the finger of God, Daniel 5:5-6.

The proverbial expression, "See the handwriting on the wall," means to come to the realization that something bad is about to happen. And that very night, king Belshazzar was killed, Daniel 5:7-31.

__410__   Three) When Jesus walked the Earth, there were fake religious leaders, just as there are now. You'll enjoy hearing Jesus tear into them in Matthew 23:1-39.

They hated Jesus because they were evil – and, because the people were following Jesus. That worried them because they were getting rich by fleecing the people. And they enjoyed having power over the people, by getting them to obey their rules, that were just superstition.

They were always trying to catch Jesus in a trap. And they would interrupt Him when He was teaching. One time they kidnapped a woman and threw her down in front of Jesus while He was teaching. They said to Jesus, "This woman was caught committing adultery, in the very act."

They asked Jesus if she should be stoned to death as the law of Moses commanded, John 8:1-5. They knew if Jesus said no, then the people would see Him as going against the law of Moses, Leviticus 20:10, and stop following Him. Or maybe those evil leaders would use it as an excuse to kill Jesus, like they killed Stephen. They wanted Jesus dead.
Acts 6:1-15; 7:1-60

If He said yes, stone her, then He could be killed by Rome, which ruled Israel at the time, and didn't let them carry out their own executions, John 18:31. But Jesus didn't answer their question. Instead, He stooped down and used His finger to write on the ground.

The Bible doesn't tell us what He wrote. Jesus is God, so, what He wrote was written by the finger of God.

Jesus knew what the law of Moses says. And in the case of adultery, both the man and the woman are to be stoned to death, Leviticus 20:10; Deuteronomy 22:22. The fact that they only brought the woman and not the man, is further proof that those brutes didn't care about the law of Moses. They dragged that woman to Jesus just to try and trap Him.
John 8:6

(continued on page 412)

412 In a death penalty case, the law of Moses says there has to be two witnesses who will testify that they witnessed the crime. And they also have to throw the first stones at the accused, Deuteronomy 17:6-7.

And, if those men knew the law of Moses, they knew that anyone who makes a false accusation must be given the punishment for the crime they falsely accused someone of, Deuteronomy 19:16-21. Jesus knew those men didn't bring the woman to Him because they were zealous for holiness. They couldn't care less. And He knew they didn't have the guts to stone her to death.

So, Jesus revealed their hypocrisy by playing along. He said, okay, you want to obey the law of Moses? Well, the law says whoever witnessed her committing adultery must cast the first stone. So, who's zealous for the law? Whose heart is truly in this? Go ahead then, pick up a stone and fling it at her. That's what Jesus was saying when He uttered His famous saying, "Whoever is without sin, cast the first stone."

Jesus didn't mean let whoever has never sinned throw the first stone. Because if He meant that, then He would be going against His own law in the Old Testament – and no one could be a witness in a court of law. There could be no juries because everyone sins. Therefore, Jesus meant whoever is not sinning regarding this matter of the woman caught in adultery, go ahead and throw the first stone.

Jesus was saying, whoever among you is not a hypocrite, whoever is not doing this to set me up. Whoever actually witnessed her commit adultery and wants to kill her to honor the law, then go ahead and throw the first stone that the law of Moses requires.

The saying Jesus used, "He that is without sin, cast the first stone," has become one of the most misused, misinterpreted, taken out of context and abused sayings of Jesus. People think it means you can't say something is a sin if you've ever committed a sin.

That's contrary to what the Bible teaches. Everyone sins, every day. Christians too. If you say you don't sin every day, you're lying, and you're calling God a liar, 1 John 1:8-10.

Yet, despite our sins, Jesus tells Christians to examine people who claim to be speaking for Him but are liars. We're to expose them as liars and warn people about them. Christians are to warn people about the penalty for sin. We're to expose deception and false teachings.

> Ezekiel 3:18-21; Ephesians 5:11-13;
> 2 Timothy 4:1-5; Revelation 2:2,6

As He waited for them to answer, Jesus again stooped down and wrote on the ground. And those phony religious leaders were pricked in their conscience. One by one, starting with the oldest, they walked away, leaving behind the woman and their alleged righteous indignation.

Jesus approached the woman. He asked her where her accusers were, and if there was no one left to accuser her. She said, "No one, Lord." And Jesus said, to her, "Neither do I accuse you. Go and sin no more."

> John 8:9-11

Jesus didn't say go and sin some more. He didn't say adultery's okay. The reason He didn't accuse her was because she called Him Lord.

By calling Him Lord, she acknowledged Him as the Lord and Savior. She was telling Him that she'd repented and wanted to obey Him now. Her faith in Him was genuine. So, Jesus forgave her sin of adultery. And, He warned her to stop committing adultery, John 8:11.

Jesus didn't come to stone sinners to death. He came to save sinners who want to give their life to Him.

> I came to search for the lost, and save them.
> I don't want them to be put to death in hell.
> Jesus, Luke 19:10

Q127) First Corinthians 10:9 says Israel snubbed Jesus before   **415**
He was born.

What did Israel do, and where is it recorded in the Bible?

416 A127) First Corinthians 10:9 says Israel snubbed Jesus before He was born. What did Israel do, and where is it recorded?

In 1 Corinthians 10:9, Christians are warned not to try God's patience, like the children of Israel did on one occasion, when God responded by sending poisonous snakes to kill them.

Israel became angry during their wilderness journey. They shouted at Moses and at God. They said, "Did you bring us out of Egypt just so you could kill us in this wilderness? There's no decent food here. There's no water. And we're tired of eating your stinking manna!"
Numbers 21:4-9

When God heard that, He sent fiery snakes to bite them. The snake's bites burned, and they were full of poison. So, the people ran to Moses. They said, "We sinned when we railed against God and against you. Ask God to take away the snakes." So, Moses prayed for the people.

God answered his prayer by telling him to do a little metal sculpting. He said, "Make a snake and put it on a pole. And anyone who is bitten will live – if they look at it." So, Moses made a shiny metal snake and put it on a pole. And when someone got bit by a snake, if they looked at the metal snake on the pole, they didn't die, Numbers 21:7-9. Jesus told us what this means:

> The snake was lifted up by Moses in the wilderness.
> And I, the Son of man, must be lifted up in the same way.
> Jesus, John 3:14

How could a snake personify Jesus? The snake represents the devil, "that old serpent," the great deceiver, who brought sin and death into the world, Genesis 2:17; 3:1-6; Revelation 12:9.

Yes, but remember, Jesus also said He will return to earth like a thief in the night, 1 Thessalonians 5:2; Revelation 16:15. That's because a thief arrives unannounced. But the comparison ends there. And Jesus had His reasons for comparing Himself to the snake in Numbers 21:8-9.
(continued on page 418)

418   God told Moses to put the snake on a pole. The word "pole" is number 5251. It means an ensign, a flag. The snake was lifted up high, where all could see. God welcomed everyone to look at the snake and live. Jesus was lifted up high, on a Roman cross, where all can see. God welcomes everyone to look to Jesus on the cross, and live – forever.

It was God who provided the antidote for the snake bites suffered by the children of Israel. All they had to do was look at the snake. And it was God who provided the antidote for sin, death, and hell. That was the sacrificial, substitutionary death of Jesus. God is teaching us that we can't save ourselves.

God gave Israel two choices. They could believe God and look at the snake and live, or refuse to look, and die. You can choose to believe God and look to Jesus on the cross and live. Or you can choose to reject Jesus, and die. Each person had to look at the snake to be saved from the snake bite. And each person has to look to Jesus to be saved from hell. You don't go to Heaven because you're a member of a certain church or denomination. Salvation is on an individual basis.

The death of Jesus was about sin. The devil is a fitting symbol for sin, seeing he was the first sinner, and the first one who seduced someone else to sin, Genesis 3:1-6,13-19; 2 Corinthians 11:1-4, Revelation 12:4. When Jesus died on the cross, He defeated sin, death, and the devil, Hebrews 2:14-15. A metal snake on a pole makes sense when we know that sin, death, and the devil, died on the same cross Jesus died on.

When Israel said, "We're tired of eating your stinking manna," they snubbed Jesus 1400 years before He was born.

Jesus said the children of Israel ate manna, bread from Heaven, but they died. Jesus said He is the Bread from Heaven that anyone can eat and live forever, and never die. The manna couldn't give eternal life, but it represented Jesus, who *can* give eternal life, John 6:30-36; 41-51. When Israel rejected the manna, they rejected the giver of life. So, they didn't have the antidote to the deadly devil bite, and they died. God sent those snakes to kill them, to make examples of them – to warn us.
                                                                                   1 Corinthians 10:11

Q128) I found no less than nine women who taught the Bible to men. How many can you find? **419**

420 A128) I found no less than nine women who taught The Bible to men. How many can you find?

At least three women taught the apostles that Jesus rose from death.

It was the women who went to Jesus' tomb, Mary Magdalene, Joanna, Mary the mother of James, and other women.

Those women taught God's Word to the apostles by reminding them that when Jesus was in Galilee, He said, "The Son of man must be delivered into the hands of sinful men, and be executed by crucifixion, and then live again after three days."   Mark 16:9-11; Luke 24:1-11; John 20:11-18

The woman at Jesus' tomb are greeted by an angel

422 (Four) Shortly after Jesus was born, Mary and Joseph brought Him to the temple, in obedience to the law of Moses, Luke 2:21-24,27,39.

There was a man named Simeon there, Luke 2:25-35.

And a woman named Anna was there too. She was at least eighty-four years old. She was always going to the temple to serve God, and fast and pray. When she saw Jesus, she gave thanks to the Lord.

And from that time, Anna talked about Jesus with anyone in Jerusalem who was eager to be saved, Luke 2:36-38.

__424__ (Five) Jesus walked to the city of Samaria. He was tired because it was a long walk. So, He sat down next to a well called Jacob's well. He was waiting for a certain woman. Jesus went there to save her soul.

John 4:1-6

When she arrived with her water pot, Jesus started a conversation. He taught her that He was the Savior, and led her to salvation, John 4:7-27.

She forgot all about the water pot she'd brought to fill with water from the well. Now she had Living Water springing up in her. She went to her city, and taught the people there about Jesus the Savior. And many of the people believed in Jesus, and were saved because of her teaching.

John 4:28-29,39

There were others who heard her speak, who went to Jesus at the well, and they too believed in Him, and were saved after listening to Him.

John 4:30,40-42

426 (Six) When the Church began, a Christian named Apollos was earnestly speaking and teaching people about Jesus. He was schooled in the Way of the Lord, and he had a powerful knowledge of the Bible, and a God-given gift to teach the Bible, Acts 18:24-25.

But Apollos only knew about the baptism that John was doing, which was only a preliminary step. Apollos didn't know about the baptism Jesus was doing, the baptism for those who receive Him as Lord and Savior, when He gives His Holy Spirit to live in them.   Matthew 3:11;
Acts 18:25

One time, when Apollos was boldly teaching in a meeting place, a married Christian couple named Priscilla and Aquila were listening carefully to what he said. And after Apollos spoke, Priscilla and Aquila took him aside, and explained the Word of God to him more accurately.
Acts 18:26

You can read more about Priscilla's ministry in the following passages, Romans 16:3-5; 1 Corinthians 16:19; 2 Timothy 4:19.

Priscilla, teacher of the Word of God, and tentmaker

428 (Seven) A good woman named Abigail married a rich fool.

Israels' king, Saul, was trying to kill God's choice for king, David. So, David fled to the wilderness with some of his loyal men. They saw the rich fool's flocks and took care of them. David asked the fool, Nabal, to help him and his men by giving them some food. Nabal cruelly said no.
1 Samuel 25:1-11

David was enraged. He said he would kill every one of Nabal's men. Someone told Abigail what David was planning. And without telling her husband, she loaded up a huge amount of food and brought it to David and his men, 1 Samuel 25:12-22.

When Abigail met David, she spoke beautifully to him. She reminded him of the way of the Lord. She persuaded him to obey God.
1 Samuel 25:23-31

Then David said to Abigail, "I give all praise and glory to the Lord God of Israel. He sent you to me today. You have God-given wisdom! I pray that He gives you all His blessings. Your godly words stopped me from seeking my own vengeance by committing murder. Because as surely as the Lord lives, if you hadn't acted quickly to come to me, I would have killed every one of Nabal's men," 1 Samuel 25:32-34.

David accepted the food Abigail brought. He told her to return home and not be afraid. And he promised not to kill her husband. When Abigail got home, she saw that Nabal was having a huge party, as though he was some sort of king. He was drunk, and feeling no pain.

So she avoided him. She waited for the wine to go out of him. And in the morning she told Nabal that she made peace with David.

Then God struck Nabal, so that his heart sank, and his body became hard as a rock. Ten days later, Nabal died. When David heard that Nabal died, he said, "Praise the Lord." And David married Abigail.
1 Samuel 25:35-42

430 (Eight) In the book of Judges, we see a familiar pattern. As soon as things went well for Israel, they started practicing evil again.

So, God would send an enemy to oppress them. That way they would learn their lesson and cry out to Him to rescue them. In Judges 4:1, Israel did evil again. This time God sent the fierce Canaanite army to attack them. And once again Israel cried out to the Lord to save them.
Judges 4:1-3

At that time in Israel, there was a prophetess named Deborah. She was the wife of a man named Lapidoth. And she lived under the palm tree of Deborah, between Ramah and Bethel. The children of Israel went to her when they needed wrongs righted, Judges 4:4-5.

When Deborah knew the Canaanites were coming, she called for a man named Barak, the son of Abinoam.

She told him, "The Lord is ordering you to take ten thousand men from the tribes of Naphtali and Zebulun at mount Tabor. And, the Lord said, 'I will make Sisera, the captain of the Canaanite army, and all his men, go to the Kishon river. I will deliver them into your hands. And you will defeat them there.'" Judges 4:6-7

But Barak said to Deborah, "I'll go if you go with me. But if you don't go with me, then I'm not going." Deborah said, "I will go with you, but you'll receive no praise for your effort, because the Lord will deliver Sisera into the hands of a woman," Judges 4:8-9.

It was a woman named Jael who killed Sisera, the captain of the fierce Canaanite army, Judges 4:15-22. Israel defeated the Canaanites. Then, Deborah and Barak sang a song of thanksgiving, Judges 5:1-31.

But it wasn't really Deborah, or Barak, or Jael who defeated the Canaanite army. It says in Judges 4:23 that God did it.

432 (Nine) Josiah was 8 years old when he became king of Judah (Israel). He was a good king, like king David before him. He obeyed God, 2 Kings 22:1-2.

One day, the high priest, Hilkiah, found something that had been lost in the temple. It was the book of the law of the Lord, the first five books of the Bible – Genesis, Exodus, Leviticus, Numbers, and Deuteronomy. God's Word had been neglected, then forgotten and lost, 2 Kings 22:8. They brought the book to Josiah. When he read it, he was so filled with sadness that he tore his clothes.

Josiah commanded Hilkiah and the scribes to ask the Lord on his behalf, and on behalf of the people, about the book of the law that was found, because Josiah knew that God was very angry because Israel did not preserve the book, and did not obey God's commands in the book.
2 Kings 22:8-13

So, Hilkiah and the scribes went to Huldah the prophetess. She was the wife of a man named Shallum, and she lived in Jerusalem.

And Huldah told them,

> Here's what the Lord God of Israel said to me.
> He said, tell Josiah that the Lord says, listen carefully.
> Because I will bring calamity to Israel.
> They will suffer all the punishments written in
> the book of the law that they rejected.
> They've forgotten Me, and worshiped idols instead.
> They provoked Me to anger by doing evil things.
> Therefore My anger will burn against them.
> And it will not be quenched.
>   2 Kings 22:15-17

Huldah also told the men that the Lord has this message for Josiah, "When you heard My condemnations in the book of the law, your heart was broken, you humbled yourself, you tore your clothes and wept. Because of that, you will die with peace of mind before I punish this place. You won't see any of it," 2 Kings 18-20.

Q129) Six times Jesus gets angry.

436 A129) Six times Jesus gets angry.

One) When Jesus walked the earth, some evil men had taken over the spiritual institutions. Jesus hated the way they oppressed the people.
Matthew 23:1-39; Mark 7:1-16

One day, Jesus went to the place of religious assembly. It was the Sabbath day. God told the nation of Israel they were to only work six days a week. The seventh day was to be a day of rest, called the Sabbath. Working was forbidden on that day. It's the fourth of the Ten Commandments, Exodus 20:8-11.

Jesus saw a man in the assembly with a paralyzed hand. The fake religious leaders had been following Jesus and watching Him closely. They'd seen Him heal people before. They had their eyes fixed on Him. If He healed this man's hand, they would accuse Him of working on the Sabbath, Mark 3:1-2. They were hoping to get Jesus killed, Mark 3:6.

Jesus told the man with the paralyzed hand to stand up. He placed the man in the middle of the room, so everyone could see him. And He asked the evil spiritual leaders, "Does the Fourth Commandment tell us to do evil on the Sabbath day by refusing to do good when the opportunity presents itself? Does God command us to let someone die on the Sabbath day and not save their life?"

The evil spiritual leaders had no answer for His question, Mark 3:3-4. Jesus looked with anger at each one of them. Then Jesus said to the man with the paralyzed hand, "Hold out your hand." The man held out his hand, and Jesus healed it. Now it was just as good as his other hand, Mark 3:5. Then those evil religious leaders held a meeting. They conspired to have Jesus killed, Mark 3:6.

The anger Jesus felt is righteous indignation. It's # 3709 in the Strong's Concordance, the Greek word *orgé*. And Jesus pitied them because they'd hardened their heart against the Savior.

__438__ Two) People were bringing young children to Jesus so He could bless them with His holy touch. But the disciples told the people to stop bothering Jesus with those children, Mark 10:13.

That made Jesus angry. He told His disciples, "Let the little children come to Me. Don't stand in their way. Heaven belongs to people who are like them. And, as a matter of fact, you'll never get to Heaven if you don't welcome Me like these little children do."   Mark 10:14-15

The King James Version says Jesus was "much displeased" with His disciples when they reprimanded the parents who were bringing their children to Him. It's one word in the original Greek, *aganakteo*, # 23, and it means to grieve, and feel pain, to the point of anger, indignation.

It means to be incensed.

440 Three) Jesus walked into God's house, the temple. He found people making money by selling cows, sheep, and doves, right inside the temple. And money changers had set up shop there too.

When Jesus saw them, He immediately got some rope and made it into a whip. Then He drove all the animals from the temple. He took the money changers cash registers and poured their coins onto the floor, and flipped over their tables. He said to those who were selling doves, "Get those things out of here. Stop turning My Father's house into a clip joint," John 2:13-16.

Then His disciples remembered what had been written about Jesus in the Old Testament, hundreds of years before Jesus was born, John 2:17.

> My zeal for Your house will consume Me.
> Psalms 69:9

The word, "zeal," is # 7068. It describes feelings that burn and boil over. Jesus was boiling over with fierce indignation because His Father was being dishonored.

__442__ Four) Jesus had some friends in the town of Bethany. They were Lazarus, and his sisters, Mary and Martha. Jesus loved them, John 11:5.

One day, Mary and Martha sent Jesus a text. It said, "Your friend Lazarus is sick," John 11:1-3.

Jesus showed the text to His disciples, and said, "Lazarus won't die. This happened to glorify God. And the Son of God will be glorified by what He's about to do," John 11:4. But Jesus didn't go to Lazarus right away. In fact, Jesus stayed where He was for two days after He got the news about Lazarus, John 11:6.

Then He told His disciples that He was going to wake Lazarus from sleep. His disciples said, "If he's sleeping, he must be feeling better." When Jesus said Lazarus was sleeping, He meant Lazarus was dead. But the disciples thought Jesus meant Lazarus was actually sleeping. So, Jesus gave it to them straight. He said, "Lazarus is dead."

And, Jesus added, "I'm glad I wasn't there. Because if I was, then Lazarus would have recovered from his sickness. But now I'm going to make you really believe that I am who I say. Let's go wake up Lazarus."
John 11:11-15

When Jesus got there, Lazarus had already been in his grave for four days, John 11:17,39. There were people at the grave, crying. Some of them said this about Jesus: "He could give sight to the blind, but He couldn't keep Lazarus from dying?" Hearing them say that made Jesus groan, John 11:37-38. Then Jesus returned Lazarus to his body.

The word, "groan," is #1690. It means someone is so angry that they express their anger like a snorting horse. It means Jesus was angry with them for saying that. And He wanted to tell them off. Jesus wasn't angry because they offended Him and hurt His feelings.

He was angry because they refused to believe in Him and receive salvation from Him. And they discouraged others from following Him. It's like the anger we feel when we hear that someone raped and murdered a child.

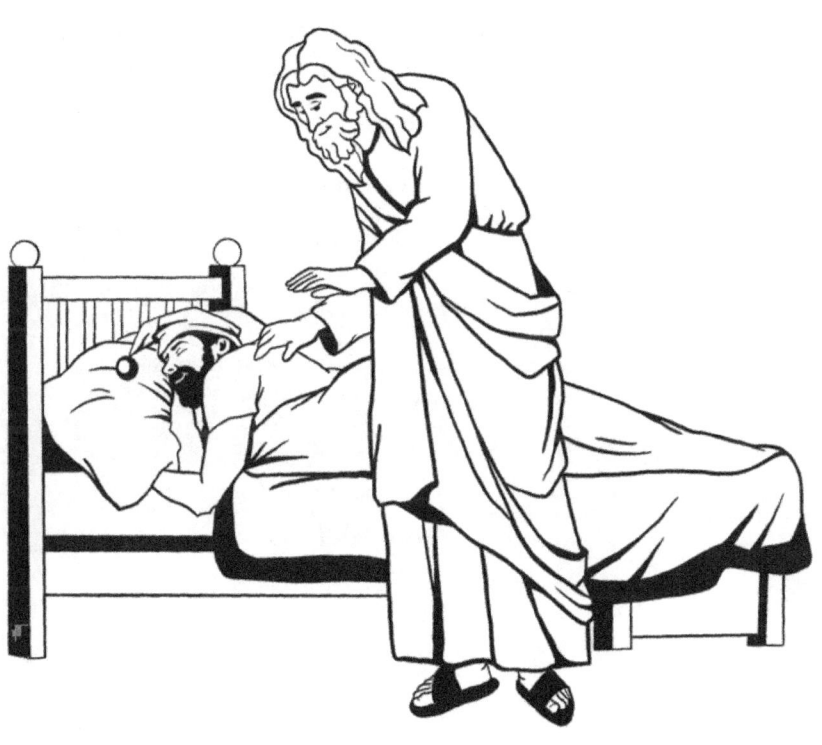

__444__ Five) Our sin makes God angry, Romans 1:18. Don't *you* feel angry when you hear about people doing evil things to children? You got that from God. You came from Him, Genesis 1:26-27, Ecclesiastes 12:7.

Jesus freely offers salvation to anyone who wants to be spared from sin's ultimate penalty. That salvation takes away God's anger.

On Judgment Day, those who refused to receive salvation will hide in mountains and caves, and behind rocks. They'll say to the mountains and rocks, "Fall on us, and hide us from the face of the One who sits on the throne. And hide us from the anger of the Lamb, because the great day of His anger has arrived, and who will be left standing?"
Revelation 6:15-17

The Lamb is Jesus, John 1:29,36; Revelation 5:1-14.

446 Six)

> Kiss the Son, lest He be angry,
> and ye perish from the way,
> When His wrath is kindled but a little.
> Blessed are all they that put their trust in Him.
> Psalms 2:12 (KJV)

TRADIDIT SEMETIPSVM PRO NOBIS. Paul. ad Philipp: V.

The inscription is Latin
It means, He gave Himself for us

Q130) Four times Jesus tells Christians to hate. **449**

450 A130) Four times Jesus tells Christians to hate.

One) Jesus told us to hate our parents, children, siblings, and spouse.
Luke 14:26

Jesus said that to upset you. If you love the truth, then you'll study the Bible to find out what He really meant. You do that by comparing Scripture with Scripture. The fifth of the Ten Commandments says, "Honor your father and mother," Exodus 20:12. Jesus taught obedience to that commandment, Matthew15:4. So, He doesn't actually want us to hate our father and mother.

Here's the answer:

> If you love your father or mother more than you love Me,
> then you're not ready to follow Me.
> If you love your son or daughter more than you love Me,
> then you can't be My disciple.
> Jesus, Matthew 10:37

Jesus wants you to love your family. But Jesus is God, your Creator. He's the Lord. You must obey Him first. And, Jesus is the Savior. So, if your family tries to stop you from following Jesus – you follow Jesus.
Luke 9:59-62

In order to get us to see that it's a matter of life and death when a family member tries to lead us away from Him, Jesus had to get drastic, and shake us up by telling us to hate that family member.

A husband must never let his wife lead him away from following Jesus.

A wife must never let her husband lead her away from following Jesus.

But wives must always strive to obey God's commandment to submit to their own husband like they submit to God Himself, Ephesians 5:22. And husbands must always strive to obey God's commandment to love their wife like Jesus loved the Church. And Jesus gave His life for her.
Ephesian 5:25

GOLDEN TEXT.—Honor thy father and thy mother, that thy days may be long upon the land which the Lord thy God giveth thee.—Exod. 20: 12.

TRUTH.—God commands us to honor our parents.

452 Two) Jesus told us to hate ourselves, Luke 14:26; John 12:25.

If you want to belong to Jesus, you have to know that you could be executed for it. The self we need to hate is our old selfish, sinful self.

Three) Jesus told us to hate evil, Amos 5:15; Romans 12:9.

This isn't like hating your family. We're commanded to love our family. We're never told to love evil. Our hatred for evil is complete hatred. God hates evil.

> If you love the Lord,
> then hate what He hates.
> Hate evil!
> > Psalms 97:10
>
> God hates lawbreakers.
> And He hates people
> who love to be cruel.
> > Psalms 11:5
>
> Christians flee from evil because we
> have a deep awe and reverence for God.
> > Proverbs 16:6

Four) Jesus was pleased with the Christians in the city of Ephesus because they wouldn't permit anyone to be among them who claimed that they were sent by Jesus, but were lying, Revelation 2:2.

And, Jesus applauded them because they hated the things that were being done by false teachers, which Jesus also hates, Revelation 2:6. Jesus commands all Christians to hate the evil done by false teachers.

De goede Harder. Ioan. x. 10.

The Good Shepherd is willing to lay down His life to protect the sheep from false teachers. But the hirelings run away to save their own life

Q131) 3 instances when those who are fleeing must not look back. **455**

456 A131) 3 instances when those who are fleeing must not look back.

One) Before God destroyed the city of Sodom, He sent two angels to rescue Lot and his family by getting them out of the city, Genesis 19:16. Then, God told them to run for their life, and not look back.
Genesis 19:17

But Lot's wife looked back, and she became a pillar of salt.
Genesis 19:26

458   Two) Jesus said that when the antichrist stands in the holy place, then Christians are to flee to the mountains.

Jesus said if you're on the roof of your house, just go. Don't take time to get things from your house. And if you're working in the field, don't even run home to get your clothes. In other words, get out now, and don't look back, Matthew 24:15-18.

And, Jesus said one more thing to illustrate the seriousness of His command that those who flee from the antichrist must not look back. Jesus said, "Remember Lot's wife," Luke 17:31-32.

In Revelation 13:11, we read of a beast that speaks like a dragon. We're told in Revelation 12:9 that the dragon is the devil. The beast has two horns like a lamb. So the beast looks like Jesus but speaks like the devil.

The beast is the antichrist, # 500. The Greek word "anti" in antichrist means "instead of," # 473. The antichrist is the devil himself, and he appears as the fake Christ. Ever since the devil rebelled against God, he's wanted to be worshiped as though he's God, Isaiah 14:13-14.

And now, as the antichrist, the devil makes his last and biggest effort to get that worship. And he will get it. The whole world will worship him, Revelation 13:8, except for God's elect, Matthew 24:24.

The antichrist looks like Jesus, but he speaks like the devil

__460__ Three) A man said to Jesus, "I'll follow You, but first I want to go home and say goodbye to my family." Jesus said, "If you put your hand to the plow and look back, then you'll never plow your way to Heaven," Luke 9:61-62.

Jesus knew the man's heart wasn't in it.

Q132) I'm thinking of two who had a conversation with the devil. **463**

One of them is in the Old Testament and the other is in the New. The devil tried to get each of them to do wrong.

One of them responded to the devil's temptations by accurately quoting Scripture. And the devil was unable to defeat that one. But the other one did not quote God accurately. They didn't stay with God's Word as it is. And the devil *did* defeat that one.

Who are the two?

464 A132) I'm thinking of two who had a conversation with the devil.

> One of them is in the Old Testament and the other is in the New. The devil tried to get each of them to do wrong.
>
> One of them responded to the devil's temptations by accurately quoting Scripture. And the devil was unable to defeat that one. But the other one did not quote God accurately. They didn't stay with God's Word as it is. And the devil *did* defeat that one.
>
> Who are the two?

The devil talked to Eve in the Old Testament, and to Jesus in the New. Eve lost. Jesus won.

One) First, Jesus fasted in the wilderness for forty days.

466 Then the devil came along and tried to and get Jesus to sin by presenting three temptations. And Jesus responded to each temptation by accurately quoting a verse from the Old Testament, Matthew 4:1-11.

In the first temptation, the devil said, "If You really are the Son of God, as You claim, then why starve? Here's some stones. Use Your power. Turn the stones into loaves of bread," Matthew 4:3.

Jesus responded by quoting Deuteronomy 8:3. He said, "It is written, people are not to just give life to their physical body by eating food. They must give life to their eternal spiritual body by eating every word that comes from the mouth of God," Matthew 4:4.

If You really are the Son of God, then turn these stones into bread

468   Then, the devil thought, *I can quote Scripture too*. But the devil misapplied an Old Testament verse to try and trick Jesus.

The devil took Jesus to the highest part of the temple building, and said, "If you're the Son of God, then throw yourself off, go ahead and jump, because it is written in Psalms 91:11-12 that God commanded the angels to surround His loved ones, and lift them up with their hands, so they won't even trip over a stone."   Matthew 4:5-6

And Jesus said, "It is also written, "Do not test the Lord your God," Matthew 4:7. Jesus quoted Deuteronomy 6:16.

470 Then the devil took Jesus to the top of a very high mountain, and showed Him all the kingdoms of the world and their splendor, and said, "I'll give You all of this if You fall down and worship me."
Matthew 4:8-9

Jesus said, "Go away, Satan. It is written, 'You must worship only the Lord your God, and serve only Him,'" Matthew 4:10.

Jesus was quoting Deuteronomy 6:13.

472 And Satan did what Jesus told him to do, he went away. Then angels came to take care of Jesus, Matthew 4:11.

474 Two) When the devil tempted Eve, he tried to put doubt in her mind about what God said, by asking her, "Is it true? Did God really say you're not allowed to eat from every tree in the garden?"

Genesis 3:1

Eve replied, "No, we're allowed to eat from every tree in the garden. But God said there's one tree we can't eat from. And we can't touch it. Because if we do, we'll die," Genesis 3:2-3. Then the devil said to Eve, "No! You will *not* die die if you eat from that tree," Genesis 3:4.

You're probably wondering why the devil said, "die die." It's because that's precisely what God said. The devil told Eve a lie when he said she wouldn't die if she ate from the tree. But while telling that lie, the devil accurately quoted the "did die" part.

In Genesis 2:17, God told Adam that anyone who eats from the devil's tree will, "die die." How do I know that? I have the four-volume Interlinear Bible, edited by Jay P. Green, Sr. It shows you every verse in the Bible in the original Hebrew and Greek. It's basically like having the original manuscripts of the Bible.

And you can see that God said, die die, # 4191 #4191, which the King James Version translates as "surely die." But Eve said God told them that if they ate from the tree, they would "die." So, Eve took away the emphasis that God put into His warning. Eve did not accurately quote that part of what God said. The devil did.

The Hebrew language draws our attention to something that's very important by repeating it two, or even three times in a row. We know the most important attribute of God is His holiness, because those around God's throne say, "Holy, holy, holy, Lord God Almighty," Revelation 4:8. Yes, the New Testament uses Hebrew idioms.

Eve told the devil that God said they could eat from the trees in the garden, Genesis 3:2. But God said they could eat eat, # 398 # 398, or as the King James Version puts it, "freely eat," Genesis 2:16. Eve left out the emphatic, second "eat." She took away from God's Word.

(continued on page 476)

The devil, disguised as an angel of light, plots evil against Adam and Eve, 2 Corinthians 11:14-15

476 Next, Eve added something to God's Word. She got it right when she said God told them not to eat from the tree. But then she said God told them not to touch the tree, Genesis 3:3. God never said that.

And what happened? Eve listened to the devil and ate from his tree, Genesis 3:6-7. Eve disobeyed God. The devil was able to defeat Eve because she didn't stay with the Word of God as it was given by God. The result was that sin and death entered the world for the first time.

The devil presented three temptations to Jesus. And the temptation he presented to Eve was also threefold. Genesis 3:6 says Eve ate from the tree because she saw that it was pleasing to look at, and it provided good food, and she perceived that eating from it would make her wise.

This corresponds to what the apostle John wrote when he told us not to love the (sinful) world, because all that's in that world is, "the lust of the flesh, and the lust of the eyes, and the pride of life."
1 John 2:15-16 (KJV)

Jesus taught by His example that the way to resist the devil's temptations is to handle the Word of God accurately. Christians are told to put on the whole armor of God, so we can resist all of the devil's temptations, which come at us like fiery darts, Ephesians 6:10-18.

Part of the armor of God is the Sword of the Spirit, God's Word.
Ephesians 6:17

There's a very important lesson in the fact that the devil quoted part of God's Word accurately when he lied to Eve. You better know the Bible.

Because the deceivers do. They'll try to dazzle you with their ability to rattle off Bible verses. But their interpretations are deadly. So, you need to be a super-serious student of the Bible.

Q133) A lamb is an animal. So, why is Jesus called a lamb? 477

__478__ A133) A lamb is an animal. So, why is Jesus called a lamb?

This is the question I used the most at my street ministry. It gave the most aha moments. Often, when I told someone the answer, I'd see their face light up. People smiled, some gasped.

Do you know about Passover? It happened when God's people, Israel, were held as slaves in Egypt. God sent Moses to free them. But the king of Egypt, the Pharaoh, wouldn't let them go. So, God sent plagues to teach the Egyptians and all the people of the world that He is God.
Exodus, chapters 7-12

God sent ten plagues. The tenth one was that all the firstborn children in Egypt would die, Exodus 11:4-7; 12:29-31.

__480__ But God told the children of Israel that no harm would come to them, Exodus 11:1-10. He told them how to mark their house.

Every family was to take a lamb. The lamb had to be perfectly healthy, with no flaws or defects. They had to kill the lamb, and put its blood on their door. God said the lamb's blood will mark the spot.

And when He sees the blood on the door, no one in that house will die. He will pass over that house. That's why it's called Passover.

Exodus 12:1-51

482 Over fifteen hundred years after the first Passover in Exodus ch. 12, John the Baptist was having a talk with some of his disciples. Then he saw Jesus walk by. And John said to his disciples, "Look at Him. He's the Lamb of God, who takes away the sin of the world," John 1:29,36.

Around six hundred years before Jesus was born, the prophet Isaiah wrote that Jesus would be led like a lamb to the slaughter, Isaiah 53:7. The apostle Paul wrote, "Christ, our Passover, was sacrificed for us."
1 Corinthians 5:7

Jesus was killed like a sacrificial lamb, like the Passover lamb in Exodus chapter 12. Jesus shed His blood when He was crucified. Christians take His blood and put it on us, so to speak, and death passes over us. We don't perish in hell. We live forever in Heaven with Jesus, John 3:16.

God told Israel that the lamb they sacrificed had to be perfect, with no defects. And Jesus was perfect because He never sinned. God is the only one who could pay for our sins, because He is the only sinless one.
1 John 3:5

> Jesus never sinned.
> We did.
> But God had Jesus die as a sacrifice for our sin.
> We can be reconciled with God because of Jesus' sacrifice.
> 2 Corinthians 5:21

The fact that the children of Israel put the lamb's blood on their door around 1500 years before Jesus was born is one thing about this question that gave people an aha moment.

It made them see that the Bible is real, and that God did all these things, and that God is the author of the Bible. That's why so many things could be prophesied and shown in types, promises, and foreshadowings, in the Old Testament, and then happen so many years later in the New Testament just as the Old Testament showed us.

Only the one true God can do that.

Q134) I asked people these three questions one after another.

One) Who was David's father?

Two) Who was Solomon's father?

Three) Who was Jesus' father?

486 A134) I asked people these three questions one after another.

One) Who was David's father?

Two) Who was Solomon's father?

Three) Who was Jesus' father?

Answers:

One) David's father.

- Jesse was David's father, 1 Samuel 17:12; 1 Chronicles 2:12-15.

Two) Solomon's father.

- David was Solomon's father (the same David as in the previous question), 2 Samuel 12:24; See 2 Chronicles 1:1-12.

Three) Jesus' father.

- God was Jesus' Father.

When Jesus prayed, He said, "Father," as He did six times in one prayer, John 17:1,5,11,21,24,25.

But what about when Jesus was dying on the cross, He said, "My God, My God, why have You forsaken Me?," Matthew 27:46. No, Jesus knew God didn't forsake Him. He was quoting David's words in Psalms 22:1, "My God, my God, why have you forsaken me?"

And in John 19:30, just before Jesus died on the cross, He quoted the last words of Psalms 22. Jesus' last words were, "It is finished." It's one word in the original Greek, the word *teleo*, # 5055. It means completed.

That's the same as the last words of Psalms 22, "He hath done this," Psalms 22:31 (KJV). It's one word in the original Hebrew, *asah*, # 6213, which means done, or accomplished.   (continued on p. 488)

488 Jesus was teaching Psalm 22 from the cross. Psalm 22 was written by David. It contains a prophecy of Jesus' crucifixion. For instance, verse 16 says, "They pierced my hands and feet." That's about Jesus. Not all of Psalm 22 applies to Jesus. The part about asking God why He has forsaken him only applies to David, not Jesus. And God didn't forsake David either. God doesn't forsake His own.
Deuteronomy 31:6-8; Hebrews 13:5

If God is Jesus' Father, then what about what happened when Jesus was twelve years old? He got separated from His parents on a trip to Jerusalem. They searched everywhere for Him, and finally found Him sitting in the temple having a conversation with the teachers.
Luke 2:41-47

Mary said to Jesus, "Why did You do this to us? Your father and me looked everywhere for You. Our hearts were crying," Luke 2:48. When Mary said, "Your father and me," she was talking about Joseph. She said Joseph was the father of Jesus.

How was Joseph the father of Jesus? Look at this: "And Jesus Himself began to be about thirty years of age, being (as was supposed) the Son of Joseph, which was the son of Heli," Luke 3:23 (KJV).

In the original Greek, the words in parenthesis, "as was supposed," is one word, *nomizo*, # 3543. It comes from the word *nomos*, # 3551, which is the word for law. The words "as was supposed" Jesus was the Son of Joseph, mean "according to the law" Jesus was the Son of Joseph.

Joseph was not the biological father of Jesus. But Joseph was the husband of the mother of Jesus. Therefore, Joseph was bound by law to serve as the legal guardian of Jesus while Jesus was a child. And Jesus was bound by law to obey Joseph as long as He was a child.

Mary told Jesus, "Your father (Joseph) and me were searching for You," Then, Jesus reminded Mary who His Father was. He said, "Didn't you know that I would be about My Father's business," Luke 2:49. His Father's business was for Him to die on a cross. And just before Jesus died on that cross, He said, "It is finished," John 19:30.

Q135) Many of the things that happened to Jesus during His crucifixion and burial were predicted in the Old Testament. Some spoke directly about what would happen to Him, and others looked like what would happen. Those predictions were written hundreds of years before Jesus was crucified.

It proves that God is the Author of the Bible.

I'll show you nine of them.

492 Q135) Many of the things that happened to Jesus during His crucifixion and burial were predicted in the Old Testament. Some spoke directly about what would happen to Him, and others looked like what would happen. Those predictions were written hundreds of years before Jesus was crucified.

It proves that God is the Author of the Bible.

I'll show you nine of them.

One) Before they crucified Jesus, they whipped and punched Him, Matthew 26:67-68; Luke 22:63-64, John 19:1.

The Old Testament said it would happen:

> I gave My back to those who beat Me.
> Isaiah 50:6

> He was wounded to make a way
> for us to be delivered from hell.
> Isaiah 53:5

__494__ Two) Before the Roman soldiers crucified Jesus, they spit in His face, Matthew 26:67. It was foretold in the Old Testament:

> I did not hide My face from insults and spitting.
> Isaiah 50:6

That was written about Jesus, six-hundred years before Jesus was born. Then why did it say, "I *did* not hide my face from … " as if it already happened? Why didn't it say, "I *will* not hide My face from … "?

It said "I did" to show the absolute certainty that it would happen.

496 Three) Then they crucified Jesus. They pierced His body by nailing Him to a cross, Matthew 27:31.

> They pierced My hands and My feet.
> Psalms 22:16

That was written hundreds of years before Jesus was born.

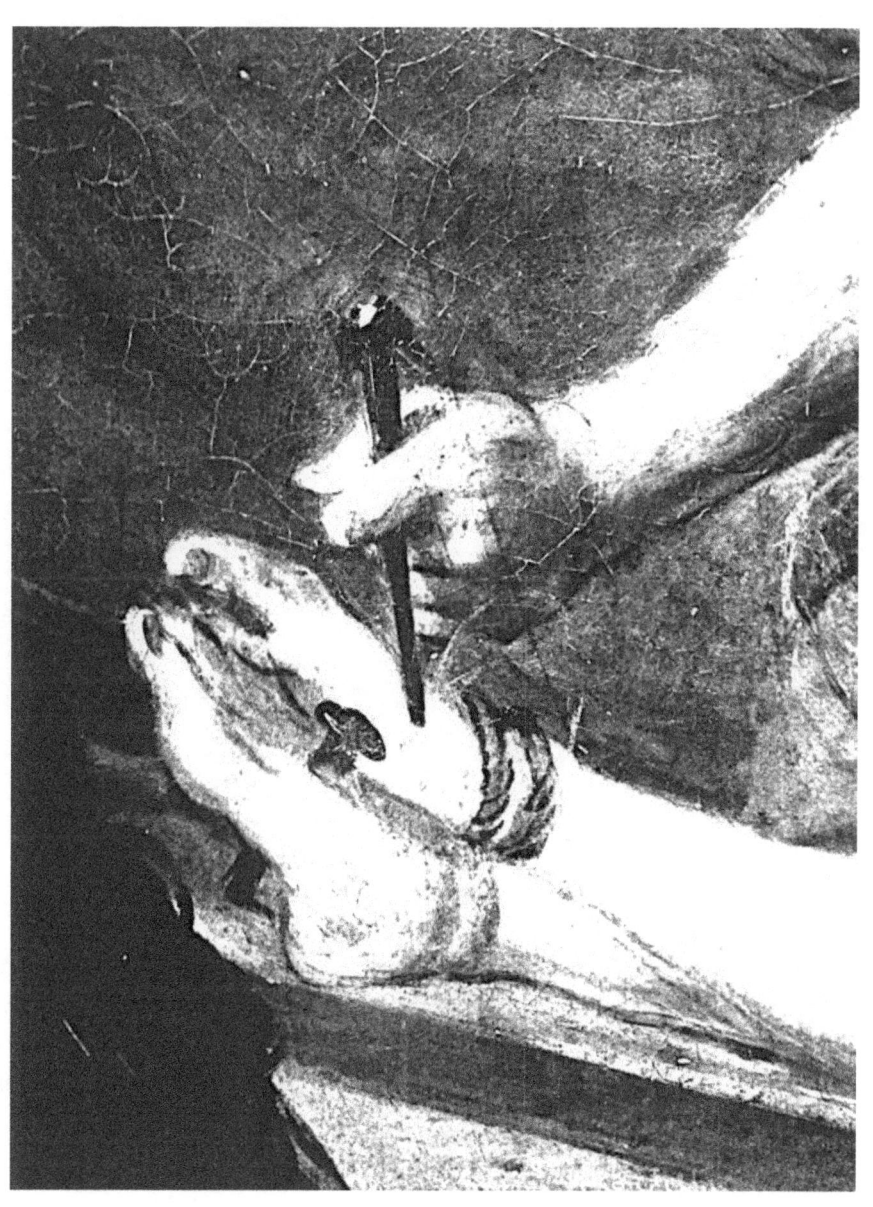

498 Four) When the Roman soldiers crucified Jesus, they stripped Him of His clothing, and divided it up among themselves. Then they threw dice to see who would get His coat, John 19:23-24.

It says in John 19:24, that this fulfilled the Scripture:

> They divvied up My garments.
> And threw dice for My clothing.
> Psalms 22:18

500 Five) It says in Mark 15:27 that Jesus was crucified along with two thieves, one on either side of Him. And Mark 15:28 says this was a fulfillment of the Scripture, where hundreds of years earlier, God had the prophet Isaiah write this:

> He was numbered with the transgressors.
> Isaiah 53:12 (KJV)

Jesus was thrown in with the criminals, as though He was one of them. But He wasn't. Jesus was innocent.

> I have sinned in that I have betrayed the innocent blood.
> Judas Iscariot, Matthew 27:4 (KJV)

> Have nothing to do with that just Man:
> for I have suffered many things this day
> in a dream because of Him.
> Pilate's wife to Pilate, Matthew 27:19 (KJV)

> I, having examined Him before you,
> have found no fault in this Man
> touching those things whereof ye accuse Him.
> No, nor yet Herod …
> Lo, nothing worthy of death
> is done unto (by) Him.
> Pilate, Luke 23:14-15 (KJV)

> We receive the due reward of our deeds:
> but this Man hath done nothing amiss.
> Said by one of the men crucified alongside Jesus, to the other man crucified with Him, Luke 23:41 (KJV)

> Certainly this was a righteous Man.
> Said by a centurion in Luke 23:47 (KJV) after he witnessed the miracles that happened when Jesus died on the cross, Luke 23:44-46.

__502__ Six) The day Jesus was crucified was the day before the holy Sabbath. The Jews didn't want Jesus and the two criminals to still be on the cross when the Sabbath day arrived, John 19:31; See Deut. 21:22-23.

They asked Pilate to break their legs. That would make it impossible for them to breathe because they would no longer be able to push up with their feet, and death would come quickly. Pilate's soldiers broke the legs of the two criminals. But when they came to Jesus, they saw that He was already dead. So, they didn't break His legs, John 19:32-33.

It was a lot of work breaking the legs. They had to use clubs. But just to make sure Jesus was dead, one of the soldiers used an easier method. He stabbed Jesus with a spear, John 19:34.

It says in John 19:36 that when the soldiers didn't break Jesus' legs, it fulfilled the Scripture that says, "Not one of His bones will be broken."

> He kept all His bones intact.
> None of them were broken.
> Psalms 34:20

When God gave Israel instructions about the Passover lamb, He said, "Don't break even one of its bones," Exodus 12:46.

Jesus is the Passover Lamb of God, John 1:29,36.

__504__ Seven) Just before Jesus died on the cross, a Roman soldier pierced His side with a spear. And immediately, blood and water came out of the wound, John 19:34.

> He was pierced because of our sins.
> Isaiah 53:5

In the KJV, that verse, Isaiah 53:5, says, "He was wounded for our transgressions." The word "wounded" is # 2490. And in Ezekiel 32:26 it's used to mean slain by a sword. The word can mean to pierce, bore.

It says in John 19:37 that when the soldier pierced Jesus in the side with a spear, it was the fulfillment of what was written in the Old Testament, and makes reference to this verse:

> I will pour out My Holy Spirit on the house of David.
> On all the inhabitants of Jerusalem, My people, Israel.
> My mercy and grace will cause them to cry out.
> They will look at Me, whom they pierced.
> And they will wail with regret.
> They will mourn like someone who lost their only son.
> They will grieve like one who lost their firstborn.
> God, Zechariah 12:10

See Revelation 1:7

506 Eight) In order that the Scripture would be fulfilled, just before Jesus died on the cross, He said, "I'm thirsty," John 19:28.

> See Psalms 22:15

So, they took a branch from a hyssop plant, and dipped it in vinegar and touched it to His lips, John 19:29.

Then, after Jesus received the vinegar, He said, "It is finished," and He bowed His head and died, John 19:30. Here's the Scripture that was fulfilled when they gave Jesus the sour wine:

> In My thirst they gave Me vinegar to drink.
> Psalms 69:21

508 Nine) A wealthy man named Joseph of Arimathaea was a good and righteous man. And he was one of Jesus' disciples.   Matthew 27:57; Luke 23:50

Joseph was a distinguished member of the city council in Jerusalem, Mark 15:43. That council was the highest court of law among the Israelites. It was that council that voted to have Jesus executed on false charges. They handed Jesus over to the Romans to be crucified.
Matthew 26:59-68; Luke 22:66-71; 23:1-34

But Joseph didn't go along with the council on that. Joseph looked forward to the day when Jesus would set up His righteous kingdom on earth, Luke 23:51. And after Jesus died on the cross, Joseph went to Pontius Pilate and asked him if he could bury Jesus' body. Pilate gave the command to let Joseph take the body, Matthew 27:57-58.

Then, Nicodemus came to help Joseph bury Jesus' body. Yes, that's the same Nicodemus who had a conversation with Jesus in John, chapter 3. Nicodemus brought around one hundred pounds of myrrh and aloes, John 19:39. There were women there too. Mary Magdalene, and Mary, the mother of Joses, Mark 15:47. Women from Galilee brought spices and ointments for Jesus burial, Luke 23:55-56.

Joseph and Nicodemus used clean linen cloth to wrap the spices around Jesus' body, John 19:40. They put Jesus' body in Joseph's own tomb, that he'd had cut into rock, Matthew 27:60. It was in a garden. No one had ever been buried there, John 19:41. Joseph rolled a huge stone to the entrance of the tomb, Matthew 27:60. What Joseph of Arimathaea did is recorded in all four Gospels.
Matthew 27:57-60; Mark 15:42-46;
Luke 23:50-53; John 19:38-42

And, six hundred years before Joseph of Arimathaea was born, the Old Testament told us that Joseph would bury Jesus in his own tomb:

>He was buried in a wealthy man's tomb.
>Isaiah 53:9 (KJV)

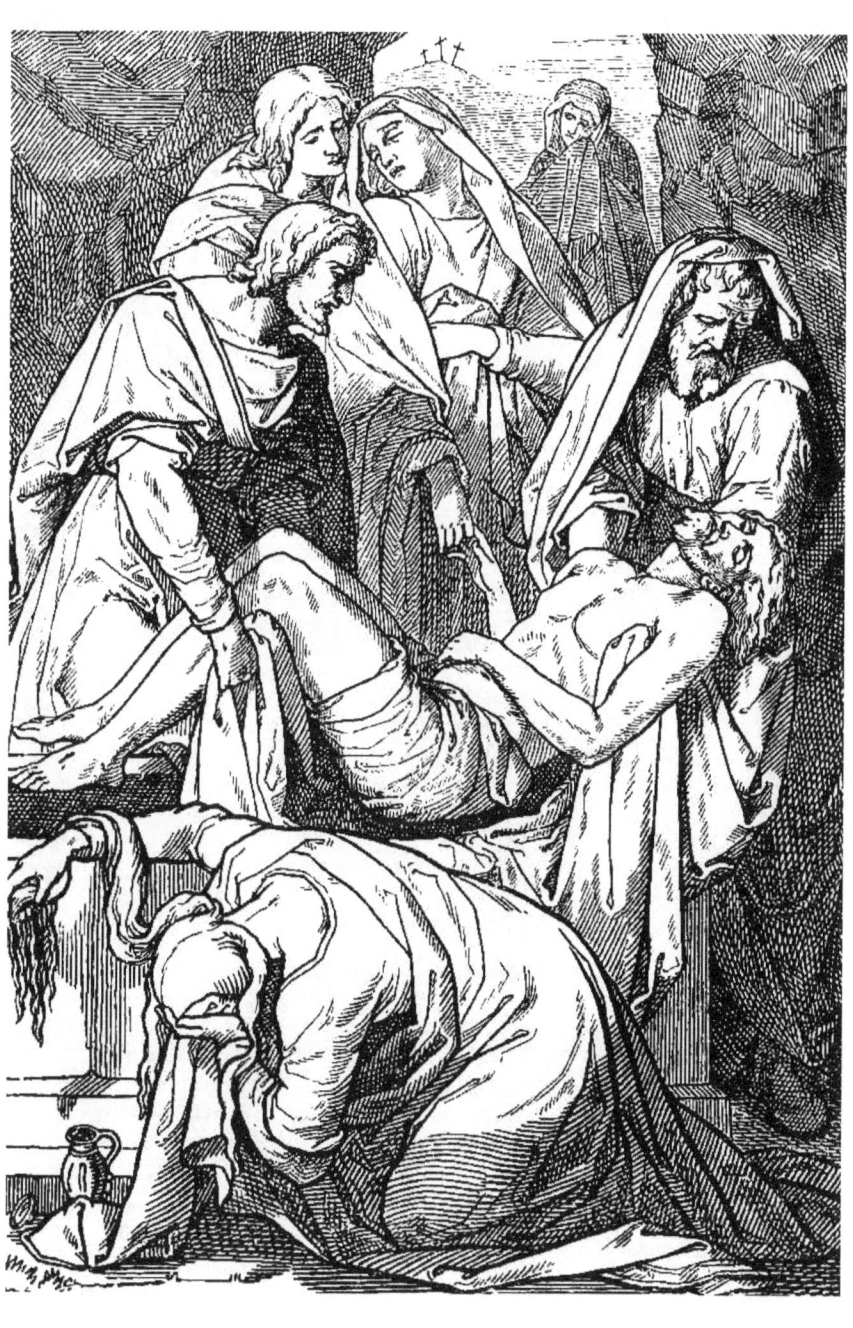

Jesus, on Judgment Day

Q136) Did Jesus say He's a thief?

512 A136) Did Jesus say He's a thief?

> Look at Me.
> Listen carefully to what I'm about to say.
> When I return, I'll show up like a thief.
> > Jesus, Revelation 16:15

Jesus deliberately horrified us by using a figure of speech called a simile to say He was "like" a thief.

Don't worry. Jesus isn't a second-story man. He compared Himself to a thief in only one way. A thief doesn't make an appointment. He shows up when you don't expect him.

That's what Jesus wants you to get from His simile.

> Stay awake.
> And watch like a hawk.
> Because you don't know which day your Lord will return.
> You need to understand this.
> If the keeper of a house knew that
> at a certain time of night a thief was coming,
> he would stop the thief from entering the house.
> Learn from that.
> You must make all the necessary preparations.
> Because I, the Son of man, will arrive at
> a time when you're not expecting Me.
> Which of you is like a faithful servant?
> He's been put in charge of a household by his boss,
> and he has faithfully fed the members of the household.
> That servant will be very happy when his boss returns
> and sees what he's been doing.
> I'll tell you something else.
> And you can take this to the bank.
> That servant's boss will put him in charge
> of everything he owns.

(continued on page 514)

514   But suppose there's an evil servant.
       And he says in his heart,
   "My boss is taking his time in returning."
       So, he starts physically abusing his fellow servants.
       And he eats and drinks with the drunkards.
       His boss will return in a day he doesn't expect,
       at a time he doesn't know about.
       His boss will break him in two.
       He will send him off to the place where the hypocrites go.
       They will weep and gnash their teeth.
              Jesus, Matthew 24:42-51

Jesus never metaphor He didn't like.

Q137) Two times a brave woman saved two good spies lives by hiding them, and then told the people who were looking for the spies that she didn't know where they were. 515

516 A137) Two times a brave woman saved two good spies lives by hiding them, and then told the people who were looking for the spies that she didn't know where they were.

One) Rahab

Jericho was the first city that Israel destroyed when they entered the Promised Land. And before they launched their attack, Israel's leader, Joshua, sent two spies into Jericho. They went to the house of a good woman named Rahab. She brought the spies up to her roof and covered them with stalks of flax to hide them.

The king of Jericho found out about the spies. He sent men to Rahab's house. They said to her, "Bring out the two men that are in your house. They've come to spy out our country." But Rahab said, "There were two men who came here, but they left. I don't where they came from. And it was dark outside when they left. So, I don't know where they went. You better get going if you hope to catch them," And the king's men went looking for the spies, Joshua 2:1-7.

Rahab's house was on the wall of Jericho. So, she used a scarlet cord to lower the two spies out her window and down the wall, and they escaped, Joshua 2:15,18. The spies returned to Joshua and told him everything, Joshua 2:16-24.

Some say Rahab sinned because she told the king's men that the spies left her place when she had them hidden on her roof. That's ridiculous. Rahab didn't sin. She was a war hero. Let me ask you this. Did God sin? Did God make Joshua sin? Listen to this:

God told Joshua to take all his soldiers and attack the city of Ai. God told Joshua not to be afraid or confused, because He will give Ai into his hands. God even gave Joshua a military strategy, Joshua 8:1-2.

Joshua followed God's plan. He commanded thirty thousand of his soldiers to go behind the city of Ai secretly, and hide, and wait for his orders, Joshua 8:3-4.

(continued on page 518)

518   Then Joshua took the rest of his army, and they stationed themselves in front of Ai. The king of Ai saw them. So, he had every person in Ai go and do battle with them. But Joshua and his army fled from the people of Ai, and ran into the wilderness. But they were only pretending. It was part of the strategy that God gave Joshua.

The king of Ai was fooled. And of course, the king didn't know about the thirty thousand Israelite soldiers hiding behind Ai. And, now there was no resident of Ai left in the city to defend it, Joshua 8:5-17.

And God told Joshua, "Take the spear that's in your hand, and stretch it out toward Ai, because I will give that city into your hand." When Joshua stretched out the spear, his thirty thousand soldiers that were hiding behind Ai, entered the city and took it and set it on fire. Then Joshua and his soldiers who pretended to flee, turned around and attacked the people of Ai from the front.

The people of Ai turned around and saw their city on fire. They were trapped. Joshua and his men killed all of them. No one escaped.
                                                                    Joshua 8:18-30

It says in James 2:25 that Rahab was justified by works when she sent the spies out another way.

What "other way" did Rahab send out the spies? It was out her window and over the wall of the city so they could escape. That was deception, a lie. And in order to carry out that deception, she had to tell the king's men that the spies left, when they were actually on her roof. The alternative was giving the spies over to the king's men.

It says in James 2:25 that Rahab was justified by what she did. Justified means she's saved, she's going to Heaven.

By the way. When James says Rahab was saved by sending the spies another way, he doesn't mean she earned her salvation by doing that. Jesus earned her salvation when He died on a cross. James means she was saved by her act in the sense that her act was the evidence that she truly believed in God, her faith was genuine. She made God happy.

Will you accuse God of sinning? Will you say He made Joshua lie? That's what Joshua did. He pretended to be scared when he wasn't. Joshua lied. But it wasn't a sin. Deception in war is a righteous act.

Rahab performed a righteous act when she told the king's men that the spies left, when they hadn't. If a madman comes to your door and asks where your daughter is, do you tell him she's up in her room?

Imagine the bravery it took for Rahab to do that. She risked her life to protect those two spies. Jesus said there's no greater love than when someone lays down their life for their friends. Rahab did that. Jesus considers her His friend, John 15:13-14.

And, Jesus put Rahab in His genealogy, Matthew 1:5.

520 Two) The woman of Bahurim

David was the king of Israel. But his son Absalom wanted to be king. Absalom used deception to win the hearts of many of the people.

Absalom wanted to kill David, 2 Samuel 17:1-4. So, David and his loyal followers fled the city, 2 Samuel 15:1-30. Two of the men who stayed faithful to David were Jonathan, the son of Abiathar, and Ahimaaz, the son of Zadok.

This is a different Jonathan than the one who was David's best friend. That was Jonathan, the son of Saul, 1 Samuel 17:57-18:1:4.

This Jonathan served as a spy for David, 2 Samuel 15:32-37, along with Ahimaaz. They were given important information about Absalom's plans. But before they could get that info to David, someone saw what they were doing, and told Absalom, 2 Samuel 17:15-18.

Jonathan and Ahimaaz managed to run away. They came to a house in Bahurim. The woman of the the house hid them in a well. She spread a covering over the mouth of the well. Then she spread ground corn on the covering so no one would know there was a well there.
2 Samuel 17:18-19

Later on, Absalom's men showed up at the woman's house. They said, "Where's Ahimaaz and Jonathan?" And she said, "They've gone over the brook of water." So, Absalom's men went and looked for them. And when they didn't find them, they returned to Absalom, 2 Samuel 17:20.

Then Jonathan and Ahimaaz came up out of the well. They went and told king David what Absalom was planning to do, 2 Samuel 17:21.

The prophet Elijah angers the king's wife

Q138) Five wives who got their husband to sin. **523**

524 A138) Five wives who got their husband to sin.

One) Eve got Adam to sin

God told Adam, "I'll kill anyone who eats from the devil's tree."
$$\text{Genesis 2:17}$$

Eve disobeyed God and ate from the tree. Then she got her husband Adam to eat too, Genesis 3:6. That's why we die, Romans 5:12.

526   Two) Sarah got Abraham to sin

>Sarah was unable to conceive. So she told her husband Abraham to have a child with Hagar, her servant, Genesis 16:1-4.

That was a sin because God made marriage to be between one man and one woman, Genesis 2:24; Matthew 19:4-6.

528 Three) Jezebel got her husband Ahab to sin

A citizen of Israel, named Naboth, had a vineyard. But the king of Israel, Ahab, wanted that vineyard because it was near his palace, and he wanted to use it for an herb garden. Ahab told Naboth that he would give him money for his vineyard, or give him an even better vineyard to replace it, 1 Kings 21:1-2.

Naboth reminded the king that the law of the Lord forbids the king from taking the land he inherited from his ancestors, Leviticus 25:23-28; Numbers 36:7-9. God hates Marxism. Naboth chose to obey God by disobeying the king, rather than disobey God by obeying the king.
1 Kings 21:3

So, Ahab pouted like a child. He wouldn't get out of bed and refused to eat. His wife, Jezebel, told him to get out of bed and eat and be merry. She said she would get Naboth's vineyard for him. Jezebel got two worthless men to tell lies about Naboth. They gave false testimony, accusing Naboth of a death penalty offense. And Naboth was executed.
1 Kings 21:4-14

Jezebel told Ahab that Naboth was dead, and Ahab took Naboth's vineyard. Then God sent the prophet Elijah to tell Ahab that dogs will lick up his blood in the same place where they licked up Naboth's blood. And Jezebel will be killed, and her body will be eaten by dogs.
1 Kings 21:15-23

And it came to pass just as the Lord said. Ahab was killed and the dogs licked his blood, 1 Kings 22:34-38.

Jezebel was killed too. And she was eaten by dogs, 2 Kings 9:30-37.

530 Four) Solomon's wives got him to sin

Solomon disobeyed God, Deuteronomy 17:17. Solomon married foreign wives, lots of them, and they got him to sin by turning his heart away from God, and getting him to worship their gods, 1 Kings 11:1-11.

> I, the Lord your God, will lead you.
> You will enter the land that you are to take.
> I will drive out many nations before you,
> including the Hittites, Girgashites, Amorites,
> Canaanites, Perizzites, Hivites, and Jebusites,
> seven nations that are bigger and stronger than you.
> I, the Lord your God give them to you.
> Do not make any treaties with them.
> Show them no pity.
> Destroy them. Wipe them out.
> Don't marry them.
> Don't give your daughter to them.
> Don't let your son marry one of their daughters.
> They'll turn your children away from following Me.
> They'll get them to worship their gods.
> Then My anger will burn against you.
> And I will destroy you suddenly.
> So, I want you to break their altars to pieces.
> Smash to bits the stone pillars they worship.
> Shatter the objects they use to worship their idols.
> Then burn all of it with fire.
> Because you are a holy people to the Lord your God.
> I am the Lord your God.
> I chose you above all the peoples of the earth.
> I chose you to be My personal possession.
> You are My special treasure.
> You weren't greater in number than all the other people.
> That's not why I chose you.
> You were the least in number.
> I chose you because I love you.
> God, Deuteronomy 7:1-8

532 Five) Herodias got her husband Herod to sin

Jesus was becoming well known because of His teachings and miracles. When the king, Herod Antipas, heard about Jesus, he said, "This must be John the Baptist risen from the dead." Herod was the one who had John the Baptist beheaded, Mark 6:14-16.

Herod didn't want to kill John. In fact, he liked listening to John speak, and he tried to protect John, Mark 6:20. You see, it was Herod's wife, Herodias, who wanted to kill John, because John told Herod that his marriage to Herodias was against God's law, Mark 6:17-19.

> It disgusts Me when a man takes his brother's wife.
> God, Leviticus 20:21

Herodias had been the wife of Herod's brother, Philip. But Herod took her from Philip and married her, Mark 6:17.

One day, an opportunity came along for Herodias to have John killed. It was Herod's birthday, so he had a party, and invited all the important people. Herodias had a daughter from before she was married to Herod. And she was at the party. She was Herod's stepdaughter.

At one point Herodias' daughter got up and put on a show, dancing in a way that made Herod and his guests very happy. Herod was so overwhelmed by her dance that he made a big mistake. He promised under oath to give her whatever she asks for, up to half of his kingdom.

She went to her mother Herodias and said, "What should I ask for?" Herodias said, "Ask for the head of John the Baptist." So she ran back to Herod, and said, "Give me the head of John the Baptist on a platter."

When Herod heard that, a wave of sadness ran through him. He knew he couldn't say no. He'd sworn an oath in front of all those important people. So, Herod sent the executioner to behead John in the prison. The executioner brought John's head on a platter and gave it to Herodias' daughter, and she gave it to her mother, Mark 6:21-32.

Q139) How do you say "without form and void" in Hebrew? **535**

In the King James Version of the Bible (KJV), Genesis 1:1-2 says:

> In the beginning God created the heaven and the earth.
> And the earth was without form, and void.
> Genesis 1:1-2 (KJV)

The Old Testament was originally written in Hebrew. My question is, how do you say, "without form, and void," in the original Hebrew?

You need to know this.

536 A139) How do you say "without form and void" in Hebrew?

In the King James Version of the Bible (KJV), Genesis 1:1-2 says:

> In the beginning God created the heaven and the earth.
> And the earth was without form, and void.
> Genesis 1:1-2 (KJV)

The Old Testament was originally written in Hebrew. My question is, how do you say, "without form, and void," in the original Hebrew?

You need to know this.

Answer:

In the original Hebrew of the Old Testament "without form, and void" is, *tohu va bohu*.

In the Strongs, it's *tohu*, formless, # 8414, and *va bohu*, void, # 922.

Tohu va bohu means a formless void. In other words, an empty wilderness, a desolate, uninhabitable place, with no order.

Q140) Did God create Earth as an empty wilderness?

540 A140) Did God create Earth as an empty wilderness?

Genesis 1:2 says:

> In the beginning God created the heaven and the earth.
> And the earth was without form, and void (an empty wilderness).
> Genesis 1:2 (KJV)

But, Isaiah 45:18 says this:

> For thus saith the Lord That created the heavens;
> God Himself That formed the earth and made it;
> He hath established it, He created it not in vain,
> He formed it to be inhabited:
> I am the Lord; and there is none else.
> Isaiah 45:18 (KJV)

In the last question we saw that in the original Hebrew, "without form and void," is tohu #8414, (wilderness) va bohu # 922 (empty).

Isaiah 45:18 says God did *not* create the Earth "vain." The word "vain," is tohu, #8414 (wilderness). Isaiah 45:18 says God did *not* create Earth as an empty wilderness. He created it it to be inhabited.

But didn't Genesis 1:2 say God created Earth as an empty wilderness? No, it didn't. It said God created the heaven and the earth, and the earth "was" an empty wilderness. The word "was" in the original Hebrew, is *hayah*. It's # 1961 in the Hebrew dictionary in the Strong's Concordance. It also appears in Genesis 19:26, which says:

> But his wife looked back from behind him,
> and she became a pillar of salt.
> Genesis 19:26 (KJV)

That's when Lot, his wife, and two daughters were fleeing from God's destruction of the city of Sodom. They were told to escape for their life and not look back, Genesis 19:17.

(continued on page 542)

Lot's wife looked back, and she "became" a pillar of salt. That word, "became," is # 1961, the word "hayah." It's the same Hebrew word that the KJV translated as "was," in Genesis 1:2, which says, "the earth was without form and void."

Let's do the math:

It says in Genesis 1:2 that God created the Earth, and the Earth was tohu, a wilderness. But it says in Isaiah 45:18 that God did not create the earth tohu, a wilderness – God created the earth to be inhabited.

Therefore "was," in Genesis 1:2, means, "became," just like it means in Genesis 19:26, which says Lot's wife became a pillar of salt. God did not create her as a pillar of salt.

God created the Earth to be inhabited, and then the Earth became tohu, an empty wilderness. How did that happen? The Bible tells us.

God created someone He trusted, who was loyal to Him. God made him powerful and beautiful, Ezekiel 28:11-19. His name was Lucifer. God gave him free will, but he used that free will to lead a rebellion against God, Isaiah 14:12-20; Revelation 12:3-4.

God responded by destroying the Earth. That's how the earth became tohu va bohu, an empty wilderness, Jeremiah 4:23-27; Genesis 1:2. Then, God created the Earth anew, beginning with His Spirit moving upon the the waters, Genesis 1:2.

That's why the Bible agrees with science, which says the Earth is billions of years old. Of course it does, it was the God of the Bible who created science.

Q141) Who's responsible for the death of Jesus?

A) Me
B) You
C) God
D) Jews
E) Jesus
F) Romans
G) Christians
H) All of the above

A141) Who's responsible for the death of Jesus?

        A) Me
        B) You
        C) God
        D) Jews
        E) Jesus
        F) Romans
        G) Christians
        H) All of the above

The answer is H, All of the above

- You and me

> It's because you and me rebelled against God.
> That's why Roman soldiers will stab Jesus.
> And hammer nails through His hands and feet.
> He will be crushed to pay for our lawbreaking.
> God will put our chastening on Jesus.
> To make peace between us and God.
> Jesus will be punched, whipped, and spit on.
> He will go through that to make a way for us to be saved.
>   Isaiah 53:5

- God

It says in Acts 2:23, that God is the one responsible for the death of Jesus. It says God handed Jesus over to the evil people who killed Him. God delivered Him into the hands of His enemies. God planned the whole thing. God knew all along what they would do to Jesus. God gave Jesus to them so they could crucify Him.

> God loves every person in the world so much,
> that He gave the life of His only begotten Son, Jesus,
> so that anyone who puts their trust in Jesus,
> will not perish in hell, but will live forever in Heaven.
>   John 3:16

- Jews

What does the Bible say?

>The Jews killed Jesus.
>1 Thessalonians 2:14-15

Well, there it is. The Jews killed Jesus. That settles it, right? No.

Jews have suffered intimidation, threats, physical abuse, and murder, from people who call them Christ-killers. The people who do that to Jews are people who choose to be ignorant. They don't want the truth. They just want to hate. They deliberately misuse Bible verses.

It was the apostle Paul who wrote those words, "The Jews killed Jesus." Here's something else Paul wrote:

>I am a Jew.
>Paul, Acts 22:3

Did Paul give Jesus over to the Romans so they'd crucify Him? No. Then who?

First of all, Jesus is Jewish. It says in Revelation 5:5 that Jesus is the Lion of the tribe of Judah. Jesus is descended from the king of Israel, David. Jesus told Pilate that yes, He *is* the King of the Jews, Luke 23:3.

Jesus came to save His people, Israel, Matthew 15:24, but the nation of Israel, as a whole, rejected their Savior, Matthew 21:42. He was rejected by the religious leaders, and they persuaded many of the people to reject Him, Matthew 27:20.

But not all Jews hated Jesus. There were Jews who loved Jesus and became His disciples, John 1:11-12. Jesus told the Jews who believed in Him that they'll prove to be His true disciples if they stay in His Word, John 8:31. That means Jews are just like everybody else.

The Jews who believed in Jesus didn't kill Him. It was the Jews who hated Jesus that killed Him. Those are the Jews Paul was talking about in 1 Thessalonians 2:14-15, when he said the Jews killed Jesus. Jews living today had no more to do with killing Jesus than you and I.

So, you speak ignorantly when you call them Christ-killers. You're committing criminal acts when you intimidate, threaten, assault, or murder Jews because you think they killed Jesus. God is angry with you. He will punish you.

You're just acting out your own sinful hatred. And you do an evil thing when you lift verses from the Bible and misuse them to try and justify your sin.

548

- Jesus

> I am the Good Shepherd.
> The Good Shepherd gives His life for the sheep.
> The Father loves Me because I lay down My life.
> Then I can take it back again.
> No one takes My life from Me.
> Instead, I lay it down Myself.
> I have the power and authority to lay down My life.
> And I have the power and authority to take it back again.
> It's what the Father commanded Me to do.
> Jesus, John 10:11,17-18

- Christians

Yes, Christians are responsible for the killing of Jesus. He had to die for our sins. We spend our life loving Him, studying the Bible, and telling the world about the salvation Jesus offers.

- Romans

The Jews weren't allowed to carry out executions because they were ruled by the Roman government, John 18:31. They wanted the Roman governor Pilate to execute Jesus. But Pilate didn't want to. He said he examined Jesus and found Him innocent, Luke 23:13-15.

The people persisted. They put Pilate in a tough spot. He knew he couldn't change their mind, and he saw that they were ready to start a riot. So, he took water and symbolically washed his hands.

Pilate told the crowd that he was innocent of the death of Jesus, and the blood of Jesus death would be on their hands, Matthew 27:24-25.

552   There were good Romans, who let God touch their heart with the truth that Jesus is God Himself, the Savior. There were three Roman military men, called centurions, who recognized Jesus as the Savior.

One time, when Jesus was in the city of Capernaum, a centurion begged Him for help. The centurion said to Jesus, "One of my servants has suddenly come down with a serious illness. He's at my house right now. He can't move and he's in unbearable pain," Matthew 8:5-6.

Jesus said, "I'll go to your house and heal him,"

The centurion replied, "Lord, I'm not worthy to have You in my house. I know You can heal him from here, just by speaking a few words."

Jesus was astonished when He heard that. The centurion's response filled Jesus with curiosity and admiration. He saw it as nothing less than miraculous. Jesus turned to the people who were watching and said He'd never seen such great faith as that shown by this centurion, not even by the people of His own country, Matthew 8:7-10.

Jesus was crucified by Romans. But it would be just as wrong and absurd to call Romans Christ-killers, as it is to call Jews that.

There were Romans who hated Jesus, and Romans who loved Jesus. Romans are just like everybody else.

554 There were two other centurions who knew Jesus was the Savior.

There was one in Caesarea, named Cornelius. He and his family were good people who respected God, Acts 10:1-2. One day, Cornelius saw an angel talking to him in a vision. The angel told him that God was pleased with him and heard his prayers.

The angel told Cornelius, "Send men to the city of Joppa, where the apostle Peter is staying, and ask Peter to come to you, and when Peter visits you, he will tell you what to do," Acts 10:3-6.

556 Cornelius called his relatives and close friends, and they all waited for Peter at Cornelius' house. When Peter walked into the house, Cornelius fell at Peter's feet and worshiped him. Peter lifted him up and said, "Stand up, I'm a man, like you," Acts 10:24-26.

558 Peter told Cornelius that his people have a rule against entering the house of someone of another nation. But God taught him in a vision that he should never call any person unworthy to receive salvation from Jesus, Acts 10:28.

Cornelius said – We're all here, in the sight of God, waiting for you to tell us all the things God has commanded, Acts 10:33.

Peter said, "I understand now that God is fair and just. He will accept anyone from any nation who respects Him and wants to obey Him." Then Peter taught everyone there about salvation through Jesus.
Acts 10:34-43

And as Peter spoke, God gave His indwelling Holy Spirit to those who heard him. The men who'd traveled with Peter from Joppa were astonished that God gave His Holy Spirit to people of another nation. Then, all those who'd received God's Holy Spirit, were baptized, they were immersed in water, Acts 10:44-48.

560 There was another centurion. He watched Jesus die on the cross.

In God's house, the temple, there was a curtain that separated the Holy Place from the rest of the temple. When Jesus died, that curtain was torn in two, from top to bottom, and there was an earthquake, and rock formations were broken apart, Matthew 27:50-53, Hebrews 10:18-20.

The centurion saw all those things, and he was suddenly filled with fear. He said, "This Man really was God's Son," Matthew 27:54.

Q142) Did Samson commit suicide?

564 A142) Did Samson commit suicide?

The book of Judges tells of a terrible time in Israel's history, when the children of Israel had no king keeping them in line. They rejected God's laws and did whatever they pleased, Judges 17:6; 21:25.

In the book of Judges, the children of Israel kept doing the same thing over and over. When things went well for them, they forgot about God and start worshiping idols. So, God would send an enemy nation to attack and oppress them. Then, Israel would suddenly remember God and cry out to Him for help. And God would raise up judges, or deliverers, to free Israel from their enemies.   Judges 3:7-9,12-15; 4:1-3;
6:1-14; 10:6-18; 13:1-5

Samson was one of those judges. God blessed him with superhuman strength. Israel had an enemy called the Philistines. God's Holy Spirit worked mightily through Samson, and he was able to single-handedly kill 1000 Philistines, using only a donkey's jawbone as his weapon.
Judges 15:14-17

566 Samson was supposed to let his hair grow because that was part of the vow of a Nazarite, Numbers 6:5, which God put Samson under from the time he was in his mother's womb, Judges 13:1-5.

Samson got involved with a woman named Delilah. The Philistines paid her to help them capture Samson. One night while Samson was sleeping, Delilah cut off his hair. Samson let Delilah deceive him. And in doing so, he broke his Nazarite vow, he disobeyed God. So, God took away his superhuman strength, Judges 16:4-20.

Did you think Samson's hair was the source of his strength? No, hair can't give a person strength. God was the source of Samson's strength. God is the one who gives strength, parts the seas, heals the sick, raises the dead, and gives sight to the blind.

568 Delilah gave Samson over to the Philistines, Judges 16:21.

570 They put him in chains, and gouged out his eyes.

572 The Philistines put Samson in prison and made him grind corn. And now, Samson's hair was growing again, Judges 16:21-22.

574 One day, the Philistines slaughtered a sacrifice as an offering to their god, Dagon. They had a big party, and they were feeling good. They said, "Our god delivered our enemy, Samson, into our hands."

Judges 16:23-24

The Philistine god, Dagon

576 As the party went on, the Philistines were feeling merry, and they thought of a way to have some fun. They had Samson brought from the prison so they could laugh at him, Judges 16:25.

But they put Samson between the two main pillars that held up the temple. And they didn't know that Samson was talking to one of the young guards who were holding him.

Samson asked the guard to let him put his hands on the pillars that support the building so he can lean on them.

There were around 3000 Philistines in the temple, men and women, all laughing at him. Samson called out to the Lord, and said, "Oh Lord, I pray that You remember me, and strengthen me. I pray only this once, oh God, so I can destroy these Philistines with one wallop, and take vengeance on them for gouging out my eyes," Judges 16:25-28.

Samson stretched out his arms and put his hands on the two main pillars that held up the Philistines' temple. He put his right hand on one, and his left hand on the other.

Samson said, "Let me die with the Philistines." He pushed with all his might. The temple of Dagon fell. And everyone in it, including Samson was killed. Samson killed more in his death than he had in his life.
Judges 16:29-31

So, did Samson commit suicide? No. He gave his life for his people. What Samson did was a picture of what Jesus would do hundreds of years later. Jesus would give his life for His people by stretching out His arms and placing his hands on either side of the cross.

But Samson committed sins. How could he be used as a picture of Jesus? The only people God can use are ones who commit sins, people like Samson and David. But they are only representations of Christ in certain aspects of their life. The sin part is incidental. All humans sin.

The only one who never sinned and never will, is Jesus.

Q143) Two who kissed Jesus.

580   A143) Two who kissed Jesus.

One) A woman who was a sinner kissed Jesus

A religious leader, named Simon, asked Jesus to have a meal with him. Jesus went to his house and took a seat, Luke 7:36. Pay close attention to what happened at this meal. Let it sink in.

A woman in that city had been unashamedly living an immoral life. She found out where Jesus was. So, she took a flask made of alabaster, that she'd filled with sweet-smelling ointment, and went to the house. She stood next to Jesus and cried. Her tears rained down on Jesus' feet until they were soaking wet.

Then she knelt down, and using her hair, she began rubbing Jesus' feet to dry them. She kissed His feet. Then she anointed His feet with the sweet-smelling ointment, Luke 7:37-38.

When Simon, the religious leader who'd invited Jesus, saw what the woman was doing, he thought to himself, "If this man really was a prophet, He would know what this woman is, and who she is that's touching Him. He would know that she's a sinner, " Luke 7:39.

Jesus is God, so He knew what His host was thinking.

Jesus suddenly spoke up and said, "Simon, I have a question for you." Simon said, "Ask it, Teacher." Jesus said, "There was a man who was a moneylender. He had two customers who owed him money. One owed him an amount equal to 500 day's wages. And the other owed him an amount equal to 50 day's wages.

"But neither of them had a way to get the money to pay him. So, the moneylender had mercy on them and forgave their debt. Now, Simon, which one of his debtors do you you think loved him more?"

Simon said, "I suppose it was the one for whom he forgave the most." And Jesus said, "You figured out the right answer."   Luke 7:40-43
(continued on page 582)

The inscription is Latin

It means, Blessed are those who mourn, because they will be comforted

That's what Jesus said in Matthew 5:4

582   Then Jesus looked at the woman, and said, "Simon, have you learned nothing from watching this woman? When I walked into your house, you didn't give Me any water to wash My feet. But she washed My feet with her tears, and dried them with her hair.

"You gave Me no kiss. But since the time she arrived here, she hasn't stopped kissing My feet. You didn't anoint My head with oil. But she anointed My feet with precious ointment.

"I tell you all this to make you understand something. I canceled this woman's debt. And it was large. I forgave her sins. That's why she has shown Me such great love. But there's someone to whom little is forgiven. And that one loves little," Luke 7:44-47.

Then Jesus said to the woman, "Your sins are forgiven."   Luke 7:48

When those who were eating with Jesus heard Him say that to the woman, they were thinking, "Who does this man think He is? He forgives sins too?"   Luke 7:49

And Jesus said to the woman, "You received salvation through your genuine faith. Go in peace," Luke 7:50.

584   Two) Judas Iscariot kissed Jesus

Judas Iscariot went to the chief priests and officers of the temple, and asked them how much they would pay him to deliver Jesus into their hands. They agreed on thirty pieces of silver. From that point on, Judas looked for an opportunity to betray Jesus.
Matthew 26:14-16; Luke 22:1-6

On the night before He was to be crucified, Jesus met with His apostles, at what is known as the Last Supper. And while they were eating, Jesus shocked the apostles by telling them, "One of you will betray Me." They asked Jesus who it was.

Jesus said, "I'll dip a piece of bread in the dish. It's the one I give it to." He gave the bread to Judas Iscariot, John 13:21-26. Judas didn't refuse the piece of bread that Jesus offered him. He took it.

Then, Satan entered Judas, Luke 22:3.

Jesus said to Judas, "What you're about to do, don't delay, do it now."
John 13:27

586 Judas left them. He rushed out the door, John 13:30.

588   Later that night, Jesus took His apostles with him to the Garden of Gethsemane, so He could pray there, Matthew 26:36.

Then Judas showed up with a mob of men sent by the chief priests and elders. The mob carried swords and baseball bats. They'd agreed on a prearranged signal. Judas said, "The one I kiss is Him. Take Him."

Judas went right to Jesus, and said, "God bless You, my Teacher," and kissed Him, Matthew 26:47-49.

Jesus said, "Are you betraying the Son of man with a kiss?" Luke 22:48.

Jesus told Judas, "Friend, do what you came to do." Then the mob put their hands on Jesus and took Him, Matthew 26:50

> Faithful are the wounds of a friend;
> But the kisses of an enemy are deceitful.
> Proverbs 27:6 (KJV)

Q144) She said this:

> I'll go wherever you go.
> Where you live, that's where I'll live.
> Your people will be my people.
> And your God will be my God.
> Where you die, I will die.
> And that's where I'll be buried.
> I pray to YHVH, the one true God, the God of Israel,
> that He make these things come to pass,
> and that nothing but death separate us.

592 A144) She said this:

> I'll go wherever you go.
> Where you live, that's where I'll live.
> Your people will be my people.
> And your God will be my God.
> Where you die, I will die.
> And that's where I'll be buried.
> I pray to YHVH, the one true God, the God of
> Israel, that He make these things come to pass,
> and that nothing but death separate us.

Ruth said that to her mother-in-law, Naomi, Ruth 1:16-17.

There was a famine in Israel. So, a man named Elimelech took his wife Naomi, and his two sons, Mahlon and Chilion, and they went to live in the land of Moab. But Elimelech died in Moab.

Then Naomi's sons married Moabite women. Chilion married Orpah. And Mahlon married Ruth, Ruth 4:10. Yes, she's that Ruth, the one the book of Ruth is named after. But ten years later both Mahlon and Chilion died, Ruth 1:1-5.

The Moabites didn't worship the one true living God. They worshiped a false god named Chemosh, 1 Kings 11:7. They were idol worshipers. God commanded the children of Israel not to marry idol worshipers.
Deuteronomy 7:1-4; 1 Kings 11:1-10;
Ezra 9:1-3; 10:1-19; Nehemiah 13:23-27

Naomi lost her husband and her two sons. And, she heard that God was once again blessing Israel with food. So, she decided to go back to Israel. Orpah and Ruth followed her. But Naomi told them to go and live in their mother's house in Moab, and she blessed them. But they said they wanted to go with her. Ruth 1:6-13

Finally though, Orpah kissed Naomi and went home to her mother. Ruth, on the other hand, wouldn't leave Naomi's side, Ruth 1:14.

594 Naomi said, "Ruth dear, your sister-in-law, Orpah, has gone back to her people, and back to her gods. You should go back too."

But Ruth said, "Auntie, please don't persuade me to turn back from following you, on account of the fact that I'm going to go wherever you go, and wherever you live, that's where I'll live.

"Your people will be my people. And your God will be my God. Where you die, I will die, and that's where I'll be buried. I pray to the LORD, the one true God, the God of Israel, that He make these things come to pass, and that nothing but death separate us," Ruth 1:16-17.

Ruth was a Moabitess, a female descendant of idol worshiping Moabites, Genesis 19:30-38. But when Ruth spoke to Naomi just now, and she prayed that God will answer her prayer, Ruth referred to God as "LORD," (KJV). if you look it up in the Strong's Concordance, you'll see that it's # 3068, which is God's sacred name, YHVH.

There are no vowels in Biblical Hebrew. God's name is YHVH. This is God's personal name. It's not used by idol worshipers. It's only used by those who believe in Him. Ruth became a believer in the true God. She's not an idol worshiper. And that's why she wanted to stay with Naomi. She wanted to take care of Naomi because Naomi was an Israelite, a believer in the true God. Ruth wanted to become an Israelite.

Yes, God told Israelites not to marry idol worshipers. But if an idol worshiper had a change of heart and wanted to love and obey the true God, then they were welcomed. And they were no less than someone who was born an Israelite. Naomi said Orpah went back to her gods. Ruth didn't go back to the gods of Moab. Ruth loved the Lord.

Exodus 12:48-50; Isaiah 49:6; 56:4-8;
John 10:16; Romans 1:16; Ephesians 2:11-13

God honored Ruth by including her in the genealogy of Jesus, Mt. 1:5.

The lesson is that anyone can turn from their sin, and turn to Jesus, and love and obey Him, and be fully embraced as a child of God.

Ruth went with Naomi to her new home in Israel. And the Lord led her to the field of a man named Boaz, where she gleaned food.

Boaz met Ruth, and blessed her with food. Then they got married.
Ruth 2:1-23; 3:1-18; 4:1-22

Boaz was Ruth's kinsman redeemer. Leviticus 25:47-49; Deuteronomy 25:5-10; Ruth 2:20

The marriage of Ruth to Boaz symbolizes the marriage of Christians to Jesus, our Kinsman Redeemer, Ephesians 5:25; Revelation 19:6-9.

www.ingramcontent.com/pod-product-compliance
Lightning Source LLC
Chambersburg PA
CBHW031424160426
43195CB00010BB/601